Baroque Brilliance

Drawings and Prints by
Giovanni Benedetto Castiglione

SANDSTEIN

KUNSTHAUS ZÜRICH

Jonas Beyer
Timothy J. Standring

Nadine M. Orenstein
Jaco Rutgers
Anita V. Sganzerla

Baroque Brilliance

Drawings and Prints by
Giovanni Benedetto Castiglione

Essays

Catalog

The exhibition and the accompanying
catalog were made possible
due to the generous support of

KYTHERA Kultur-Stiftung, Düsseldorf
WOLFGANG RATJEN STIFTUNG, Vaduz
Tavolozza Foundation

as well as of another foundation which
prefers to remain unmentioned.

Lenders and Acknowledgments

Her Majesty Queen Elizabeth II

Staatliche Museen zu Berlin: Michael Eissenhauer
The Devonshire Collections, Chatsworth: Alice Martin
Hessisches Landesmuseum Darmstadt: Martin Faass
National Galleries of Scotland, Edinburgh: John Leighton
Städel Museum, Frankfurt am Main: Philipp Demandt
Musée d'art et d'histoire, Geneva: Marc-Olivier Wahler
Hamburger Kunsthalle: Alexander Klar
The Jan Krugier Foundation, Lausanne: Tzila Krugier
The Courtauld, London: Ernst Vegelin van Claerbergen
Victoria and Albert Museum, London: Tristram Hunt
Musée des Beaux-Arts de Lyon: Sylvie Ramond
Staatliche Graphische Sammlung München:
Michael Hering
Beaux-Arts de Paris: Jean de Loisy
Bibliothèque nationale de France, Paris:
Laurence Engel
Fondation Custodia / Collection Frits Lugt, Paris:
Ger Luijten
Musée du Louvre, Paris: Laurence des Cars
Museum Boijmans Van Beuningen, Rotterdam:
Sjarel Ex
Staatsgalerie Stuttgart: Christiane Lange
Musée Jenisch Vevey: Nathalie Chaix
Albertina, Vienna: Klaus Albrecht Schröder
Graphische Sammlung ETH Zürich: Linda Schädler

For their generous support of the exhibition,
we would also like to thank all the private lenders
who wish to remain unnamed.

For their suggestions and keen help and support in
preparing this exhibition, our thanks also go to:

Rhiannon Ash, Jacqueline Austin, Alexandra Barcal,
Katrin Bellinger, Andreas Beyer, Maryline Billod, Alexandra Blanc, Julia Blanks, Kinga Bódi, Peter F. Carls, Delphine
Charpentier, Martin Clayton, Tina Dähn, Natalie Danford,
Christine Delaunoy, Daniela Dölling, Laura Donati,
Anne Drouglazet, Albert J. Elen, Mieke Fransen, Ciara
Gallagher, Achim Gnann, Peter Goop, Ketty Gottardo,
Stéphanie Guex, Barbara Guidi, Mechthild Haas, Kazusa
Haii, Lindy de Heij, Corinna Höper, Victor Hundsbuckler,
Mariska de Jonge, Tim Knox, Dagmar Korbacher, David
Lachenmann, Céline Le Bacon, Peter Lukehart, Michael
Matile, Ariane Mensger, Christof Metzger, Sara Mittica,
Larry Mizel, Emmanuelle Neukomm, Charles Noble,
Nadine M. Orenstein, Francesco Passaro, Line Clausen
Pedersen, Susanne Pollack, Lauren Porter, Alisia Robin,
Brigitte Robin-Loiseau, Christian Rümelin, Jaco Rutgers,
Xavier Salmon, Silvia Salvini, Lena-Catharina Schneider,
Vanessa Selbach, Anita V. Sganzerla, Martin Sonnabend,
Andreas Stolzenburg, Cécile Tainturier, Nader Tewelde,
Annette Weisner, Johannes Willms, Christel Winling,
Kurt Zeitler.

Foreword

Giovanni Benedetto Castiglione epitomizes the qualities that make the art of the Baroque so fascinating: the cult of genius and artistic inspiration, an exuberant display of splendor, the ambition to overwhelm viewers with a surfeit of sensory stimuli. Yet to this day he remains the great unknown among Italy's acclaimed artists. The most recent major exhibition on Castiglione, devoted to his graphic works, posited him aptly enough as a "lost genius." Influenced by Titian's legacy and the contemporary production of Gian Lorenzo Bernini and Nicolas Poussin – all artists whose works he studied extensively – Castiglione forged his own path, leaving behind a body of work that is both intensely individual and strikingly original.

It was Castiglione's sovereign mastery of draftsmanship – at least on par with his mastery of painting – that made him so exceptional among seventeenth-century artists. He set down his subjects on paper with tremendous facility – often using an idiosyncratic technique: he mixed his pigments with linseed oil, probably after being inspired by the nimbly executed oil sketches on panel that were a specialty of Peter Paul Rubens and Antony van Dyck. This enabled him to produce an astonishing spectrum of expressive qualities depending upon the brush's degree of saturation: from flowing, painterly lines all the way to flecked, expressive strokes. The rapidity with which he guided his oil-soaked brush across the paper prompted contemporaries to characterize his method as "grazioso" (graceful) and "facile" (straightforward). Far from being derogatory, however, the term *facile* was meant as praise of his consummate virtuosity.

Castiglione's brush drawings resemble tiny "drawn paintings." They were notably not preparatory sketches for paintings, but rather autonomous works in their own right – which explains why they were so esteemed by prominent artists such as Giovanni Battista Tiepolo and Jean-Honoré Fragonard, as well as being coveted by legendary art connoisseurs such as Count Francesco Algarotti and Zaccaria Sagredo. Even today, the largest inventory of Castiglione's drawings remains in the best of hands, namely in the collection of Queen Elizabeth II: fifteen of the most attractive sheets in the present exhibition were loaned from the Royal Collection at Windsor Castle. Loaned works have also arrived from other splendid collections, among them the Devonshire Collections in Chatsworth House and the Collection Frits Lugt in the Fondation Custodia in Paris. We are grateful that so many were willing to entrust their treasures to us!

On par with Castiglione's drawings are his print works. With enigmatic and eccentric subjects drawn from the Apocrypha or mythology, his etchings stand in the tradition of the *capriccio*, and depict scenes staged amidst a variety of *all'antica* objects that seem to have been strewn almost randomly throughout the picture space, abandoned to the elements.

Castiglione often experimented with novel techniques, developing, for example, what has since become known as the monotype, by painting directly on a printing plate and transferring the image onto a new support, usually in a single impression. This approach allowed him to achieve dramatic chiaroscuro effects and a distinctive mixture of painting and drawing that was uniquely characteristic of the art of his time.

Castiglione was a master of seemingly effortless execution, simulating ease while overcoming great technical challenges – and it is this that makes him a virtuoso in the best sense of the word. We are thus delighted to invite all of you to join us on a journey of discovery – not only in the first Castiglione exhibition to go on show in a German-speaking country in living memory, but also in this catalog publication, which vividly charts Castiglione's position in the history of art. Many thanks to our authors Jonas Beyer, Nadine M. Orenstein, Jaco Rutgers, Anita V. Sganzerla and Timothy J. Standring, for their probing and provocative contributions. For the initial impetus leading to this publication and exhibition, we are indebted to the curator Jonas Beyer, who launched this project together with Timothy J. Standring, assisted judiciously by Martina Ciardelli. With her accustomed efficiency, Franziska Lentzsch assumed responsibility for overall coordination. The KYTHERA Kultur-Stiftung, Düsseldorf kindly provided financial assistance for shipping, the WOLFGANG RATJEN STIFTUNG generously helped with catalog costs, while additional support came from the Tavolozza Foundation and a further unnamed foundation. My heartfelt gratitude goes to all of them, as well as to the team at the Kunsthaus for their tremendous commitment to this undertaking. And now, let us immerse ourselves in and marvel at the biography and creative oeuvre of an artistic genius: Giovanni Benedetto Castiglione!

Christoph Becker
Director, Kunsthaus Zürich

Essays

Notes on a Lost Genius: Giovanni Benedetto Castiglione

Timothy J. Standring

Giovanni Benedetto Castiglione, called Il Grechetto, was a voluble and charming bon vivant, a spendthrift who cherished both the good life and an ostentatious wardrobe and yet was prone to shifts of mood and violence, which led Nicolo Pio to proclaim that he was more feared than loved.[1] At one point, he destroyed a commissioned painting in a fit of rage, shouting that Doge Giovanni Battista Lomellini of Genoa would never again have the opportunity to acquire a painting by him. Shortly thereafter, he departed for Rome dressed in "the Armenian style" in a long tunic, pretending he was from Greece.[2]

He had reason to be proud. After all, clients beyond Genoa also sought out his works, including Carlo II Gonzaga, Duke of Mantua and Montferrat, who enticed him to move to Mantua. Little wonder, then, that his fame during his lifetime spread north of the Alps and throughout Europe. Cornelis de Bie praised him along with twenty-three other Italian painters in his compendium *Het Gulden Cabinet*, published in Antwerp in 1662.[3] Abbé Michel de Marolles initiated Castiglione's posthumous fame as a printmaker, by listing forty-seven etchings by the artist in his *Catalogue de Livres d'Estampes et des Figures en Taille douce*, published in 1666.[4] In addition to being imitated and copied considerably by his contemporaries, Castiglione's most significant artistic impact north of the Alps occurred later, in France, with such artists as Boucher and Fragonard.[5] And many of the early collectors of his drawings may have learned about him from information provided by some of his earliest biographers, though their narratives do little more than provide perfunc-

tory lists of his most commonly known works that were available to be seen at the time. Save one or two exceptions, these biographies are largely uncritical of the facts they record; they really don't take issue with any of the details of the artist's life, nor do they necessarily focus on how his life events may have impacted his art. While virtually all remark on his verve of execution and brilliantly vivid coloring – a core feature of Castiglione's art – only one biographer, Nicolo Pio, drew attention to what an irascible mean-spirited person the artist was.[6]

Castiglione began his career as a painter of animals and of journey scenes with the patriarchs of the Old Testament but, after arriving in Rome by the early 1630s, he expanded his repertoire to include narrative scenes with mythological subjects. In his effort to re-fashion himself as a painter-philosopher during the late 1640s and early 1650s, he produced etchings of erudite content that appealed to European humanists.[7] Following Salvator Rosa's marketing strategy, he was happy to have his etchings circulated as a means of attracting clients.[8] That may have been the case of works such as *Circe with the Companions of Odysseus Transformed into Animals* (cat. 68) and *Diogenes Searching for an Honest Man* (cat. 65), as well as *The Entry of the Animals into the Ark* (cat. 73) and *The Nativity with God the Father and Angels* (cat. 72), among others. From 1645 onwards, following the success of his *Adoration of the Shepherds* altarpiece for the Spinola family chapel in Genoa (fig. 1), he continued to receive commissions through intermediaries for altarpieces for religious orders.[9] Completed in 1650 in Rome, his

Fig. 1
Giovanni Benedetto Castiglione
The Adoration of the Shepherds
1645 · oil on canvas · 398 × 218 cm
Fondazione Spinola, Chiesa di San Luca, Genoa

Immaculate Conception with Saints Francis of Assisi and Anthony of Padua (fig. 2) received great acclaim when exhibited in Palazzo Verospi on the Corso (where the Romantic poet Percy Bysshe Shelley would later reside, in 1819). It was subsequently installed in the suppressed church of the Capuchin order at Osimo in the Marche, which was built in 1648 and dedicated to the *Immaculata*.[10] Stardom followed throughout the early to mid-1650s when he was sporadically in and out of Genoa. He received commissions that continue to hold our attention, such as his allegorical statement *Omnia Vanitas* (cat. 32), which is closely related to two painted versions.[11]

Although Genoese guidebooks mention an abundance of Castiglione's paintings among collections and churches throughout Genoa, Francesco Algarotti and Consul Joseph Smith, to name but two influential connoisseurs of many, may have contributed more to spreading his fame throughout the eighteenth century.[12] From 1743 they started commenting favorably on the artist's drawings in the collection of Zaccaria Sagredo in Venice, where some of the sheets were so prized that they were shown in frames under Venetian glass.[13] Indeed, writers referred to Castiglione's graphic handling as lively and freewheeling, a style which often displayed the kind of unfinished appearance that would be increasingly admired throughout the nineteenth century.[14] Contemporary painters today who encounter his work for the first time pronounce similar remarks.

Castiglione's formative years in Genoa were fortuitous. He first frequented the studio of Giovanni Battista Paggi, whose print collection, library, and *quadreria* provided a wealth of images from which he could draw throughout his artistic journey.[15] Important, too, was Paggi himself, whose theoretical and literary interests introduced the crucial concept of *ut pictura poesis* — that a painting is a mute poem — to the novice, who quickly learned to become a storyteller. This was the locus where Castiglione would have been exposed to the new sciences, to libertinage, and to tracts of hermeticism, all of which may underscore the meaning of a number of his works.[16] Giovanni Andrea de Ferrari and Sinibaldo Scorza provided him with additional technical training in painting and printmaking. However, the genesis of his many sheets — drawn or painted (it is difficult to say which), using boar-bristle brushes with oils on unprepared paper — may stem from his exposure to examples by Paggi himself, or by Rubens and Van Dyck in other Genoese collections. Additionally, an embarrassment of riches among Genoese collections and churches complemented his introduction to theory and practice during his formative years. He benefitted from the unparalleled breadth and depth of

Fig. 2
Giovanni Benedetto Castiglione
The Immaculate Conception with Saints Francis of Assisi and Anthony of Padua
1649–1650 · oil on canvas · 367 × 221 cm
Minneapolis Institute of Arts

Italian painting originating in Venice, Florence, Bologna, Rome, and Milan, as well as Flemish and Dutch canvases from northern Europe.

This was just the beginning of a career that would take him throughout the Italian peninsula on peripatetic journeys not unlike those of the patriarchs he painted. He traveled from Genoa to Rome to Naples, back to Rome, back to Genoa, and then on to Mantua, Venice, and Parma. Throughout his peregrinations, he would have encountered figures from the eastern part of the Mediterranean world, many of whom he would paint throughout the rest of his career. Biographer Ratti summarized Castiglione's tutelage as stemming from varied sources yet processed intuitively to suit his own needs.[17]

Fig. 3
Giovanni Benedetto Castiglione
Jacob's Journey
1633 · oil on canvas · 98 × 134 cm
Private collection

His trajectory toward success during his early years, however, was not without its hurdles. His early works inspired by popular prints after works by Bassano and painted with Flemish naturalism did little to advance his career in Rome. To contemporaries whom he aspired to emulate, such genre scenes of transhumance intended to portray episodes of the lives of Abraham, Jacob, Laban, or Rebecca would have been considered low on the hierarchy of subject matter. He sold most of these paintings early in his career as "ready-for-sale" pictures – exemplified by his first known signed and dated painting, *Jacob's Journey* (1633; fig. 3) – to relatively modest collectors on the open market rather than as bespoke pieces.[18] He became known for his specialization in patriarchal journey pictures, a commercial practice not uncommon for fledgling artists such as

Castiglione in Rome at the time. Without question, such repetitions became the most common subject of Castiglione's entire oeuvre, a subject that allowed him to pay the bills, but whose success also seems to have been a hindrance to his ambitious artistic agenda. Having attended some sessions in 1633 and 1634 at the Accademia di San Luca in Rome, it must have grated on Castiglione to have been referred to as "the artist who paints scenes of the journey of Jacob."[19] Additionally, he was insulted in an improvisational farce performed in the home of Conte Nicola Soderini. The actors mocked how he had to draw "with the assistance of *spolveri* [powder]," referring to the use of "cartoons" with holes pricked through the paper, so that one could blow chalk dust through them to transfer the outlines of an image. In effect, he was accused of being such an inept draftsman that he could only draw by copying mechanically, with the assistance of a template.[20] This exhibition shows otherwise.

In addition to mastering drawing with oils and pen and ink (see pp. 56–57), he also faced challenges throughout the mid- to late 1630s when adapting source material. His *Saving of the Infant Pyrrhus* (ca. 1635–1640; cat. 41) lacks the narrative rationale of Poussin's version; while his remake of Titian's *Sacred and Profane Love* (ca. 1635; cat. 39) fails to capture the original's visual allegory.[21] Though such dry-brush drawings fail to convey the crux of each work's emotional content, they are not without merit, as their captivating painterly surfaces amply demonstrate. His intention, as formulated over the decade from the mid-1630s to the mid-1640s, was to focus on his inimitable handling, which became ever more robust as he gained confidence and adapted such mark-making in subsequent works. His challenge was to sustain his painterly bravura in works that blurred painting with drawing whilst appropriating motifs and, in some cases, entire compositions from others, be they altarpieces by Guido Reni or Giovanni Lanfranco, or a funerary monument (1633–1644) to Countess Matilda by Gian Lorenzo Bernini (cat. 40).[22] Furthermore, from the late 1640s to mid-1650s, he set himself the challenge of attaining the same psychological intimacy and technical intensity demonstrated in Rembrandt's prints.[23] To Castiglione, emulation did not necessarily mean appropriating the source's content. Instead, his intention was to impart a novel inflection – *his* novel inflection – to such source material.

His drawing that depicts the moment when Circe turns one of Odysseus' men into an animal (cat. 27) was inspired by two woodblock illustrations that accompany commentary on Ovid's *Metamorphoses*.[24] Such an allegorical image was intended as an admonishment about sensual temptation, perhaps because it was thought that Odysseus distinguished himself from his bestial companions through his rational and temperate power to abstain from Circe's seductive powers. Equally powerful is the work's dry-brush handling that blurs the distinction between a sketch and an accomplished *modello*, for it shows Castiglione purposefully harnessing his manner to enhance the story. In a similar fashion, his drawing depicting Apuleius transformed into a donkey (ca. 1660; cat. 26) was based on a print by an artist known as the Master of the Die as an illustration (after Michiel Coxie I) for an edition of *The Golden Ass* (fig. 4). Here, the author Lucius Apuleius has been transformed into an ass and is seen listening to an elderly woman recounting the story of Cupid and Psyche to the rich young maiden Charite.

Fig. 4
Master of the Die, after Michiel Coxie I
Apuleius Changed into a Donkey, Listening to the Story Told by the Old Woman, from **The Story of Cupid and Psyche as Told by Apuleius**
1530–1560 · engraving · plate: 19.7 × 23.5 cm
The Metropolitan Museum of Art, New York

Castiglione's work habits, however, primarily involved reusing his own motifs and compositions. There is one instance of a full sheet of his sketches in the National Museum of Art in Oslo (fig. 5) in which he played with possible configurations using small thumbnail sketches. Following these smaller compositions, he would bring pen and ink to paper to create larger studies with the same verve as his dry-brush drawings. His two landscape sketches (cats. 1, 2) suggest that like his contemporaries Claude and Poussin, he too delighted in drawing landscapes for their own sake without any iconographic accoutrements. His *Historical Scene: Three Figures Kneeling before a Sovereign and Soldiers* (cat. 30) and two studies of *Circe* (cats. 28, 29) also convey the same scribbly lines and delicate crosshatches, fields of stipple, flicks, and dashes found in his etchings – all constituting one of the most individual graphic styles among his contemporaries.

Like the nineteenth century French artist Edgar Degas, he also worked with motifs across media, which may offer a clue as to how Castiglione chanced upon producing *his* first monotypes – unique prints produced by drawing an image directly on an inked copper plate, pressing a sheet onto it, and pulling both through a printing press.[25] He is sometimes acknowledged as one of the first to produce

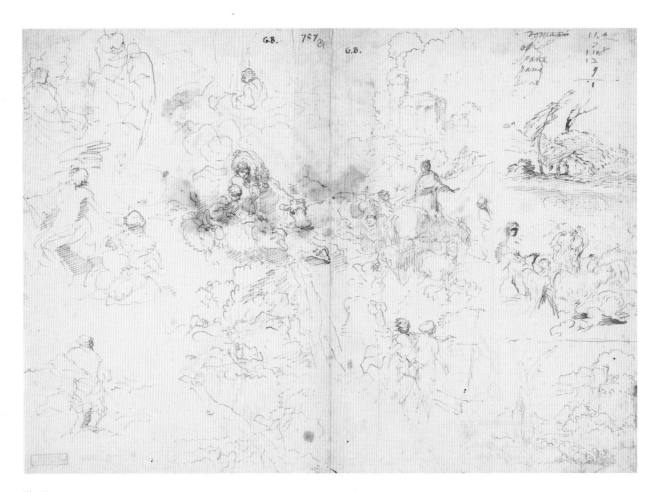

Fig. 5
Giovanni Benedetto Castiglione
A Sheet of Sketches
ca. 1650 · pen and ink on paper · 28.9 × 41 cm
Nasjonalmuseet for kunst, arkitektur og
design, The Fine Art Collections, Oslo

this type of print, a feat never acknowledged during or after his lifetime until the twentieth century. In fact, in some instances, the term "monotype" is a misnomer since an artist like Degas would often pull another, second impression of the same inked plate, which is called a "ghost" or "cognate" of the first pull. Here Castiglione produced two images of *The Nativity with Angels and God the Father* – the first located at the Bibliothèque nationale de France, Paris (cat. 49), the second in the Royal Collection at Windsor Castle (cat. 50) – and included similar motifs in an etching (fig. 6) representing the same subject, as well as in two drawings.[26] Working with such layered transpositions and repetitions of motifs and compositions became fundamental to Castiglione's process, especially when his workshop began to include other artists, such as his brother,

Salvatore, and his son, Giovanni Francesco.[27] With such intimate workshop activity it is clear that questions of attribution regarding his drawings will continue to challenge connoisseurs.[28]

By the late 1640s and early 1650s, Castiglione preferred to produce significant mythological, religious, and especially allegorical works, the latter of which sometimes address his patrons in Mantua. Two pen-and-ink drawings connected to an allegory in honor of the ruling couple of Mantua (cats. 34, 35) constitute his thoughts for two different paintings that address the theme. They also relate to his allegorical print *The Genius of Castiglione* (cat. 67), which proclaims his creative spirit.[29] However, he was not content to broadcast estimation of himself solely through allegory. He had a habit of including his self-portrait[30] and did so in

Fig. 6
Giovanni Benedetto Castiglione
The Adoration of the Infant Christ
ca. 1645–1650 · etching · plate: 28.4 × 20.4 cm
Harvard Art Museums/Fogg Museum

Fig. 7
Giovanni Benedetto Castiglione
**Studies of Various Heads and a Figure
of Victory**
ca. 1645–1650 · pen and brown ink, and
wash on beige laid paper · 26.6 × 37.4 cm
Gallerie dell'Accademia, Venice

a number of paintings as well as in an etching (cat. 55) and a drawing.[31] Neither was he averse to including other figures that appear to be portraits, as seen in two versions of *Deucalion and Pyrrha*. As a result, it should not come as a surprise that he was also known as an active portraitist in oils, as well as in works on paper, as demonstrated by the tightly drawn *Head of a Youth in a Turban* in red chalk (cat. 44), the dry-brush drawing for *A Potentate, Carrying a Mace and a Sword, Half Length* (cat. 43), and a pen-and-ink sketch of *Studies of Various Heads and a Figure of Victory* (fig. 7).[32]

Castiglione's highly personal works, drawn from an array of diverse iconographic and stylistic sources, distinguish his art from that of his contemporaries. By insisting

on packaging his allegories with a farrago of animals, still life objects, sculpture, and figures such as maenads, satyrs, and nymphs, among others, all set in pastoral landscapes, he was, in fact, proclaiming artistic preferences wholly his own. After all, his works found inspiration not only from common literary and visual sources, but quite possibly from monuments specially constructed out of ephemeral materials for courtly festivities, as well as from tableaux vivants from the early days of opera. His relationship with Ottavio Tronsarelli, as one possible example, may be the link between the artist and some literary and operatic figures of the early seicento. Tronsarelli was a prominent Roman poet who once wrote a poem about one of Castiglione's paintings, *Saint Peter Crying in the Wilderness*, and many libretti published in his *Drammi musicali*, which were of considerable influence on Poussin.[33] The pyramidal arrangement of the figures in many of Castiglione's drawings brings to mind the ephemeral monuments made out of papier-mâché, plaster, and other like materials for temporary festivals and often paraded in processions around courtyards or down streets.[34] His brother, Salvatore, wrote about one such event in a pamphlet, *Copia di lettera scritta dal Signor Salvator Castiglione … circa l'entrata, & accoglienze fatte … alla Regina di Svecia* (Turin, 1656).[35]

Giovanni Benedetto Castiglione found delight in rendering images of magical transformations inspired by Ovid's tales and, notwithstanding the different subjects he treated, he nonetheless found a common thread of meaning among them, suggesting – as many during his time had – that a melancholic temperament was somehow the result of sorcery. Additionally, he implied that earthly endeavors vanished in the face of the inevitability of decay and death. The excitement of metamorphosis, however, came with a dose of dark musings on existence, which might have been precipitated by the traumatic turns of his life. Given his frequent movements throughout Italy, his inability to settle in his native Genoa or participate in the community affairs of the many cities in which he is said to have lived, as well as the fact that he died relatively impoverished, it is surprising that he possessed any degree of fame in his lifetime. And yet, he did. And still does today.

Thanks are offered to Natalie Danford, Alisia Robin, and Peter Lukehart for their assistance with this essay, which is dedicated to the memory of Carl M. Williams.

1 Pio 1977, p. 177. **2** Ibid., pp. 177–178; the anecdote, based on notes by Mariette who used Pio as his source, was repeated by Marius Chaumelin, in Chaumelin 1865, pp. 3–4. **3** De Bie 1661, p. 305. **4** De Marolles 1666, p. 40. Blanc 2017, pp. 121–137; 233–281. **5** Exh. cat. London/Denver/Fort Worth 2013, pp. 161–163; see also Blunt 1954. **6** Soprani 1674, pp. 223–226; Félibien 1725 [originally published between 1666 and 1685], vol. 3, p. 518; Baldinucci 1681–1728, pp. 534–535; Mariette 1744, p. 6; Dezallier d'Argenville 1745–1752, vol. 1, pp. 379–382; Pio 1977, pp. 177–178; and Ratti 1768–1769, vol. 1, pp. 308–315. The most up-to-date study on Castiglione is exh. cat. London/Denver/Fort Worth 2013. **7** See essay in this volume by Anita V. Sganzerla, pp. 35–43. **8** On Castiglione's marketing strategies, see exh. cat. London/Denver/Fort Worth 2013, pp. 78–93. **9** Magnani 1990, cat. 14, pp. 118–121; and exh. cat. Washington 2020, pp. 208–209. **10** Gabrielli 1955, pp. 261–266; and Waterhouse 1967, pp. 5–10. **11** Standring 2021, pp. 483–490. **12** Ratti 1766. See exh. cat. London/Denver/Fort Worth 2013, pp. 161–163 for a summary of Castiglione's critical fortunes. **13** Binion 1983, p. 396. **14** Watelet and Levesque 1791, vol. 5, p. 66. See also Sohm 2001; and Suthor 2021. **15** On Paggi, see Lukehart 1987. **16** See Lavaggi, 2000/2003, pp. 237–243; Sposato-Friedrich 2014; Magnani 2014, pp. 215–234; Montanari 2020, pp. 1–32. **17** Ratti 1768–1769, vol. 1, p. 309. **18** Standring 2011b. **19** Lukehart 2015, pp. 45–58. **20** Exh. cat. London/Denver/Fort Worth 2013, pp. 34–37. **21** Ibid., figs. 13, 15. **22** Ill. Wittkower 1955, pl. 58; on Castiglione and Lanfranco, see Spione 2020. **23** See essay in this volume by Nadine M. Orenstein, pp. 45–53. **24** One woodblock image is by Pierre Vasse (or du Vase) in an edition of Alciati's *Emblemata* of 1550 under the section "Luxuria" or licentiousness with the warning "Cauendum à meretricibus" (beware [the consequences of visiting] prostitutes); the other is Virgil Solis illustration of the woman in the Frankfurt editions of Ovid's *Metamorphoses* of 1563; the fleeing lad from the latter a motif clearly harking back to Caravaggio's *Martyrdom of Saint Matthew* (1599–1600), San Luigi dei Francesi, Rome. **25** See essay in this volume by Jonas Beyer, pp. 23–33. **26** Nationalmuseum, Stockholm, inv. 1605/1863, and Albertina, Vienna, inv. 49.673. **27** On Castiglione's workshop, see exh. cat. London/Denver/Fort Worth 2013, pp. 138–141. **28** Ibid., p. 121. **29** Ibid., p. 69. **30** These comprise the small figure to the far left in both versions of *Jacob's Journey*, 1633 (private collection, signed and dated, formerly Marco Grassi collection, and Museo del Prado, Madrid, inv. 86); the man to the left, pointing upwards, in the *Entry of the Animals in the Ark* (ca. mid-1640s, Museu Nacional de Belas Artes, Rio de Janeiro, inv. 1789); and the figure wearing a skullcap, lower left, inscribing the base of a ceramic pot in *Deucalion and Pyrrha*, signed and dated 1655 (Denver Art Museum, inv. 1998.39). The Stockholm drawing is illustrated in exh. cat. Philadelphia 1971, cat. 68. **31** Nationalmuseum, Stockholm, inv. 1602/186. **32** In addition to portraits of the Genoese senator Marc'Antonio Rebuffo, Giovanni Battista Raggi, and Cardinal Lorenzo Raggi, he etched images of Agostino Mascardi and Anton Giulio Brignole Sale, signed and dated 1641. On Castiglione's caricatures, which deserve to be better known, see Cheng 2008, pp. 237–238. **33** Exh. cat. London/Denver/Fort Worth 2013, pp. 37–38. See also Montanari 2015. **34** Nussdorfer 1998, pp. 439–464. **35** Castiglione 1656.

Genium Io.
Benedicti
Castilionis
Ianuen~
Inu.Fe.

Reciprocities: The Relationship between Etching and Monotype in Castiglione's Work

Jonas Beyer

They are still in use: those pleasingly simple, almost primitive printing techniques still practiced by contemporary artists today. One of the most straightforward is taking a counterproof from a still-wet, freshly painted or inked piece of paper by simply pressing a blank sheet against it. There are countless examples of artists (all the way up to Andy Warhol[1]) using this process which willingly assigns chance a hand in the outcome. Paper-to-paper printing is also something that even young children are familiar with.

Only slightly more elaborate is the use of a printing plate, to which the color is applied. In contrast to conventional printing processes, the plate, or matrix, remains unscored and is not engraved or etched with any permanent marks. More importantly, the application of ink to a smooth plate that is then pulled through a press along with a sheet of paper results in only a single truly saturated print. The occasional second impression, or second pull, uses remnants of ink left on the printing plate and thus necessarily turns out paler, which is why it is termed a "ghost impression." These unique prints run counter to the general notion of printmaking as a way of churning out identical reproductions of one and the same image. This process of producing one-off prints is called monotyping, and the resulting prints are monotypes.

A few years ago, the Wallraf-Richartz-Museum in Cologne showed an exhibition devoted to the counterproof – *Der Abklatsch. Eine Kunst für sich*[2] – which also included monotypes. The title could not have been more apt, for the phrase "eine Kunst für sich", translates as "an art apart" or "an art for its own sake," indicating either an art form that is difficult to classify and that oscillates between media or an art form that has its end in itself.

As this article explores not only Giovanni Benedetto Castiglione's etchings but also the monotype technique which he is widely believed to have invented,[3] this self-referential dimension – of being "an art for its own sake" – is always implicit. And indeed, this dimension could be acknowledged as the key to classifying Castiglione's monotypes within his graphic oeuvre. In Castiglione's art, the techniques of monotype and etching must be considered in direct juxtaposition, not only because he often treated the same subjects in both techniques, but also because one process can be understood as a consequence of the other.[4]

The Genius of Castiglione

It has already been noted elsewhere that the sheer abundance of iconographic allusions invests Castiglione's etchings with a decidedly hermetic character. "The iconographic clues," as the Munich curator Kurt Zeitler writes, "carry within them the germ of the dissolution of a 'readable' content."[5] This does not, of course, absolve art historians

Fig. 1
Detail of cat. 67

from taking the trouble—as indeed they have always done—of tracking down the iconographic references in Castiglione's work. After all, for the educated collector who fancied himself as a gentleman-scholar, a large part of the appeal of prints of this kind lay in the intellectual pleasure of decoding the artist's oblique references. One could pit one's erudition against that of one's fellow literati.[6] But for all that, and despite numerous interpretations, there is still no conclusive explanation of the meaning of what is probably the artist's most famous print—*The Genius of Castiglione* (cat. 67 and p. 22). Without wishing to add a further interpretation to the pile, I would like to point out just a few details in this print that are relevant to the argument of this article:

Behind the young man reclining in the foreground rises a richly decorated stone pedestal which supports the bust of a woman.[7] The trailing end of the veil that is draped around her head casts a shadow on a face in relief on the pedestal below. The similarity between this face and representations of the head of Medusa is striking.[8] What else could be the purpose of shadowing this face, if not to deprive the Medusa's gaze of its power to turn onlookers to stone?

Once sensitized to the theme of stone, we notice the enigmatic smile playing on the lips of the woman, making

the ancient stone appear animate and touched by life. Less striking, but still visible to the naked eye, are the faces of satyrs that can be made out on the sacrificial stone altar in the left middle ground (fig. 1). Far from being purely decorative applied moldings, they seem to emerge one moment from the febrile tangle of etched lines as latent images struggling to take form, only to disappear again the next.

With regard to the shadowed face of the Medusa, we might therefore conclude that what is playing out in this scene is not petrification but, conversely, vivification of the inanimate stone. The putto in the background indicates that this miraculous feat must be recognized as the artist's achievement. The glorious fanfare of the putto's trumpet is not directed at the figure of the youth farther below.[9] Instead, it seems to be squarely aimed at the sacrificial altar and thus at the life unfolding in the stone.

In the overall context of the print, these are details well worth pointing out, for the meaning of this sheet is likely to amount to more than the mere sum of its iconographic parts. We must take account of the fact that something is actually happening in this etching.[10] Interestingly, in Cesare Ripa's *Iconologia* the plumed beret, seen here on the reclining young man's head, is associated with the personification of *capriccio*[11] and emblematic of multifaceted creativity. Such a connection seems all the more likely precisely because it is the genre of the *capriccio* that allows the artist to treat seemingly portentous motifs in a playful manner without necessarily intending the viewer to be able to decode them conclusively. Although the enigmatic motifs induce us to pore over the prints—lest we miss a significant detail—over the course of such close observation, the eye is increasingly drawn to the intrinsic qualities of the individual elements and their virtuoso handling. It is worth noting that not only did the genre of the *capriccio* first emerge as a graphic form in the prints of Jacques Callot, but one of its other distinguishing features was also that the technical sophistication in producing a *capriccio* often became an end in itself as soon as the focus shifted from the subject to the question of the subject's handling.[12]

The term *capriccio* thus gave the artist some leeway to disregard the rules of classic art theory and to let their own imagination run wild. This article proposes that Castiglione's monotypes should be considered within the context and genre of the *capriccio*.

The Monotype as an Arena
for Artistic Spontaneity

If the deliberately enigmatic iconography of Castiglione's etchings does indeed carry within itself the "germ of the dissolution of a 'readable' content," and if the overload of riddles increasingly shifts our focus from the "what" of the representation to the "how" of its realization, then the opposite extreme would be the removal of any prompts whatsoever on how to read the image through the radical reduction of explanatory visual clues. This, too, is something Castiglione achieved – notably in the medium of the monotype.

According to the art historian Augusto Calabi, the original purpose of Castiglione's monotypes was to remedy a shortcoming of his own etchings: The artist, Calabi explains, sought to achieve a more pronounced chiaroscuro effect than was attainable by means of his etcher's needle, which produced infinitely varied shades of gray but did not lend itself to the rendering of velvety blacks or strong contrasts between passages of light and dark. His quest for a viable alternative eventually led him to develop the monotype process.[13] Such an explanation may suffice to explain the origins of the monotype technique. In view of the dominance of grayish half-tones in many of Castiglione's etchings, it even makes for a plausible argument. However, given that the chiaroscuro effect of his etchings improved over time, it fails to answer the question as to why Castiglione rendered the same subjects – among them several night scenes – also in the monotype technique at a later point in his career.[14]

The monotype lends itself to nocturnes insofar as the uniform inking of the plate ensures that a saturated darkness prevails before the image is worked up. Castiglione first rolled black printer's ink all over the plate and then scraped the areas intended as highlights out of the viscous film of ink. To carve out the lights, he did not have to cut into the plate itself, but only the layer of ink on it. Thanks to this comparatively effortless process, the energy of the artist's hand movement translated directly into his mark-making. Castiglione's monotypes thus represent a sophisticated attempt of combining visible mark-making with dramatic chiaroscuro. The artist's focus was on the dynamic white streaks and patches, which stand out against the dark untreated ground.

Many of Castiglione's monotypes can only be titled with any degree of confidence because an etching of the same subject has come down to us. The title of the monotype *The Entry of the Animals into the Ark* (fig. 2), for example, is derived from a corresponding etching (cat. 73), the composition of which features a similar grouping of animals surging toward the left. In the etching, too, the artist's primary focus was evidently on the animals themselves, which Castiglione skillfully grouped in the foreground of the composition. Of particular note is his decision to draw attention to the white of the blank sheet through the prominent placing of the horse. While the background of the etching offers a glimpse of

Fig. 2
Giovanni Benedetto Castiglione
The Entry of the Animals into the Ark
1650–1655 · monotype · 24.6 × 35.3 cm
The Devonshire Collections

Noah's ark as the goal toward which the animals are striving, the monotype homes in on a much more tightly cropped moment of the event. The animals' destination is missing, so that the viewer might not even identify the print as a depiction of a biblical event. The monotype has no actual "vanishing point," and the procession of animals could be continued ad infinitum on either side of the sheet.

Another striking feature of the monotype is that the lines drawn in the ink capture light bouncing off the bodies of the animals, defining them without necessarily tracing their entire outline. The partial illumination of the creatures provides sufficient information to read those passages that remain in darkness as belonging to the bodies and not to the dark background. However, the quality of the mark-making can also be appreciated independently of its mimetic function. Instead of being completely absorbed into the form they conjure, the lines stake a claim to validity in their own right and reference the way in which the image was created. In general, we can state that with the transfer of a subject from etching to monotype, the subject tends to become secondary to the technical execution. This phenomenon can be observed throughout the artist's graphic oeuvre and will be brought to the fore by a closer examination of the correlation between etching and monotype.

Temporary Eternity

The print *Temporalis Aeternitas* has come down to us not only as an etching (cat. 66 and fig. 3) but also as a monotype (fig. 4). In the etching, the protagonists are surrounded by ruins of ancient monuments. Four figures gather around an inscribed slab on the base of a tomb which is illuminated by a torch held by a small figure with his back turned to us. The somewhat oxymoronic title, *Temporalis Aeternitas*, stems from the figures reading the inscription on the tomb. Translated as "temporary eternity," it can be read as a reference to the transience of all earthly endeavors.[15]

Two of the figures are crouching, the one directly in front of the tablet is carefully studying the inscription, tracing it with his index finger, while the other seems to be transcribing it into a book, as if to stave off oblivion by quickly creating a written record of it. The monumental vestiges of past grandeur, which form part of the typical repertoire of a Baroque *capriccio*, lend themselves perfectly as a backdrop that underlines the tenor and content of the etching. The juxtaposition of weathered, ruined monuments and the epitaph suggests that the print's underlying subject is the steady decline of human accomplishments

over time that we can only stem by perseverance and steadfast remembrance.

As already noted in *The Genius of Castiglione*, here, too, the artist played with the idea of the vivification of stone. Not only do sculptures seem to move when they are contemplated by the light of a flickering torch,[16] but we also get the impression that the male figure closest to the picture plane is a sculpture brought to life, that he is in fact just descending from his pedestal, which, on closer inspection, turns out to be the base of a column. As in Castiglione's *Genius*, we are invited to study all the elements of the composition closely, however enigmatic their configuration may initially appear.

The gradations of brightness are superimposed like a kind of filter over the overall composition, which is fully articulated and resolved even in the darkest parts. To darken the areas of the image that remain in shadow, Castiglione applied additional cross and parallel hatching over the tight network of hooks and scribbles, but the values of light and shadow are differentiated enough to define the objects in their customary materiality. That's how the etching was done – how does the corresponding monotype compare?

Torchlight Dramaturgy

In the monotype (fig. 4) the unmediated juxtaposition of light and dark results in snatches of detail being presented from a partly withheld bigger picture, with the dramatic lighting giving the objects a somewhat fragmentary appearance. In contrast to the etching, here the distribution of light and dark follows the logic of the flickering torchlight alone. This has freed the artist to choose the objects to which the viewer's attention should be drawn – irrespective of whether they are essential or secondary to the picture's content. Even objects that would have been considered merely decorative within the framework of academic aesthetics are now charged with meaning by the lighting and thus made to carry the same weight as motifs vital to the narrative.

Castiglione deliberately avoided casting the setting of the scene in full light. This not only leaves us in the dark about its dimensions, it also deprives us of any perspectival clues that would allow us to fathom the pictorial space, which would, in turn, make us forget the materiality of the picture surface. Instead, the technical aspects of the execution take center stage, so that we cannot help but perceive the monotype as a work that took shape on the picture surface, in a process that was as rapid as it was calculated.

Fig. 3
Giovanni Benedetto Castiglione
Temporalis Aeternitas
1645 · etching · plate: 30 × 20.3 cm
Harvard Art Museums/Fogg Museum

Fig. 4
Giovanni Benedetto Castiglione
Temporalis Aeternitas
1645 · monotype · 29.6 × 20.1 cm
The Royal Collection / HM Queen Elizabeth II

That all these strategies were deployed to draw attention to the virtuoso handling of the image is particularly evident in one detail: Castiglione has placed his signature on the stone slab, where the Latin motto is written in the etching, thereby declaring himself as the central theme of the picture. After all, it was the artist who has singlehandedly transformed that fleeting moment, caught in the flickering light of a torch, into a thing of permanence by fixing it on paper. The feat of capturing a transitory state is thus irrevocably attributed to the artist, whose signature in the monotype could hardly have been placed in a more conspicuous spot, especially in view of the theme – all eternity – of the Latin inscription which it replaced. The print thus plays with the reference to the author and presents itself as an art form that is entirely self-referential.

Light as a Carrier of Meaning

Complementing his torchlit night scenes, Castiglione's religious images allow us to interpret the dark pictorial ground of the monotype on a metaphorical level that goes beyond the merely nocturnal. Thus, although no one is likely to misinterpret a work such as *The Creation of Adam* (fig. 5) (for which there is no corresponding etching) as a profane night scene, the dominant overall darkness is perfectly plausible in terms of the metaphysics of light. The idea of life emerging from light is conveyed with compelling directness in this work. Indeed, the emergence of Adam from amorphous primordial darkness is tantamount to an act of creation, which the artist – likening himself to God the Creator in a way – not only made the subject of his print but was also able to perform with his own hands by means of the monotype process.[17]

Similarly, no comparable etching has come down to us for the monotype *Christ on the Cross* (cat. 54). Once again, everything seems to be designed to invest the light with religious meaning as it stands out against the dark ground. The slumped body of Christ, hanging heavily from the cross, contrasts with the dynamic energy of the rays of light radiating into the darkness. Obviously, they should be read as an emanation of divine light and thus as triumph over death. The dark background of the image, in turn, recalls the words in Luke 23:44–46: "And it was about the sixth hour, and there was a darkness over all the earth until the ninth hour. And the sun was darkened, and the veil of the temple was rent in the midst. And when Jesus had cried with a loud voice, he said, Father, into thy hands I commend my spirit: and having said thus, he gave up the ghost."

Fig. 5
Giovanni Benedetto Castiglione
The Creation of Adam
late 1640s · monotype · 30.3 × 20.3 cm
The Art Institute of Chicago

Painterly Prints

Thus far we have looked at only one of the two monotype techniques – namely the subtractive, or so-called dark-field manner, in which the design is scratched out of a film of ink rolled onto an otherwise featureless plate. However, albeit somewhat more rarely, Castiglione also made use of the arguably easier reverse process. He also produced monotypes in the additive, or so-called light-field manner, in which the design is drawn in ink directly on a clean plate. How the actual print will turn out, after plate and paper have been pulled through the press, is never entirely predictable and always holds an element of surprise for the artist.

The Metropolitan Museum of Art in New York probably had precisely this process in mind when it mounted *The Painterly Print*, an exhibition devoted to the monotype.[18] There can be little doubt that artists had long harbored a desire for a printmaking process that boasted painterly qualities. The chiaroscuro woodcut, developed in the early sixteenth century, had already aimed to simulate broad washes and fluid tonal gradations by combining line and tone blocks. However, despite its technical sophistication, a sixteenth-century chiaroscuro woodcut will always be seen as seeking to emulate the aesthetics of another medium. By contrast, it is much more difficult to distinguish Castiglione's brush drawings from his light-field monotypes.

But if the monotype process yields only a single satisfactory print, why choose to go down the print route instead of painting directly onto the paper in the manner of an oil sketch? The most compelling explanation is probably that it is easy to manipulate the ink on the polished plate but almost impossible to make substantial changes once ink or paint is applied to paper. Working on the plate thus leaves room for experimentation and draws attention to the process of image-making rather than just the resulting image itself. Moreover, the plate could be wiped clean and made ready for another monotype. What kind of subjects were best suited to treatment in the painterly light-field manner?

Castiglione's "Oriental Heads"

The light-field technique is used to particular effect in Castiglione's "Oriental Heads" – examples can be found in the collection of the Victoria and Albert Museum in London and the Royal Collection at Windsor Castle. In the Windsor print (cat. 45), the artist used the brush to render different surface textures to convincing effect – from the precious jewelry and fur collar to the rough imperfections of the face. Castiglione scratched individual lines into the painted parts of the plate to render the light bouncing off the pleats of the turban or the bristly white hairs of the beard and fur coat (thus combining light- and dark-field processes). He also applied additions to the print, retouching certain passages around the beard with oil paint and finishing the background with a brown wash.

These carefully composed bust-length figures bear witness to the artist's keen sensitivity for purely aesthetic questions. Uncommissioned and therefore not subject to any demands from a patron, the *tronie*-like portraits of anonymous models provided Castiglione with an opportunity to demonstrate his singular inventiveness, virtuosity, and ability to work in a variety of styles. The exotic character heads can thus be regarded as a direct manifestation of his creative imagination. Here, too, unsurprisingly, parallels can be drawn with his etchings.

Serial Heads

Castiglione produced one large and one small series of etchings of men in exotic headdresses (cats. 58–63). With these series of highly sophisticated portrait etchings, Castiglione presented himself as Rembrandt's equal,[19] able to produce a rich chiaroscuro with nothing more than an etcher's needle. And it is from this dense web of frenetic lines that his "Orientals" seem to emerge, creating the impression that the figures and the shadows that frame them had grown, inseparably, out of one and the same tangle of lines.

The etching of a turbaned man from the small series of portraits (fig. 6), for example, does not even show the man's beard in full. The right half of his body is only rendered in a few faint lines, as if the strong light coming in from the right had erased any more detailed definition at this point. Stripped of their function of rendering dense volumes, his lines begin to assume a life of their own. While Castiglione used lines in some parts of the print to suggest shadows, in the lower third of the image and on the sides of the sheet they became a vehicle for spontaneous scribbling, outlining a horse's head and a sketch of a hand in the lower left corner and a second, much smaller head of an "Oriental" on the upper left beneath the artist's signature. The sheet thus creates the impression that the artist had playfully and lightly guided his etching needle across the plate and that even the central subject had grown out of a continuous flow of spontaneous artistic inspiration.

The focus is always on the sophistication of execution, on artistic brio, most certainly in the monotypes – but also in the etchings. This also explains why some of Castiglione's figures are seen turning away from the viewer. Instead of merely appreciating each individual physiognomy, our eye is meant to delight in the realization of the image as a whole. A few of the "Orientals" are cast in deep shadow to draw attention to the vibrating layer of dense strokes that takes possession of the figure (cat. 62).

Significantly, Castiglione's decision to treat a motif in serial form to demonstrate his capacity for virtuosic variety within repetition suggests that the Oriental heads are rooted in the tradition of the *capriccio*. Here, monotype and etching ultimately achieve something very similar: in both techniques – one essentially painterly, the other resolutely graphic – the artist sought to render the various textures of skin, fur, and fabric with utmost subtlety. Art and artistic virtuosity are obviously the central theme of these works; the motifs merely provide the artist with an opportunity to display the full gamut of his creative powers.

Fig. 6
Giovanni Benedetto Castiglione
Bearded Old Man with Head and Eyes Lowered,
Wearing a Turban with Fur, from **Small Oriental Heads**
late 1640s · etching · plate: 11.2 × 8.3 cm
Private collection

Fig. 7
Giovanni Battista Tiepolo
Six People Watching a Snake,
from **Scherzi di Fantasia**
1742–1744 · etching
plate: 22.7 × 17.7 cm
Graphische Sammlung ETH Zürich

Fig. 8
Detail of fig. 7

Castiglione's Legacy

It should have been sufficiently clear that far from merely being casually playful experiments, Castiglione's monotypes are fully fledged and ambitious works in their own right. Fruitful echoes have been identified between etchings and monotypes — especially with regard to their *capriccio*-like qualities. What already seems to be inherent in Castiglione's etchings, namely the deployment of alienating effects — be it through the dense accumulation of iconographically complex visual symbols or through the technical sophistication of his highly original treatment of an established subject — is consistently mirrored or even heightened in the monotypes. Many of the monotypes can best be described as linear extracts of what had already been carefully and laboriously worked out in an etching, but now executed with obvious impulsiveness and by taking full advantge of the possibilities of swift variation.

Castiglione's capricious idea of entangling the viewer in impenetrable spatial contexts only to have them light upon his signature, as in the monotype *Temporalis Aeternitas* (fig. 4), may even have inspired no less an artist than Giovanni Battista Tiepolo, who very discreetly scattered multiple signatures across one of his *Scherzi di Fantasia* (fig. 7), in such a way that the individual letters of his name merge seamlessly into unconnected cursory marks, requiring the viewer to recalibrate their gaze again and again (fig. 8).[20]

Even if Tiepolo's etching was not directly inspired by Castiglione's monotype *Temporalis Aeternitas* (which, notably, was in the collection of Zaccaria Sagredo in the Venice of Tiepolo's day[21]), a very similar phenomenon can be observed in it. These enigmatic pictures, which captivate us in their mysterious, elegiac mood, make us want to strike upon some deeper meaning. But as soon as we engage with this mysterious cosmos of weathered *all'antica* monuments and venerable figures, as soon as we take a closer look at the scattered props, we always come upon the artists themselves, whose sophisticated manner bears the unmistakable mark of their hand. They were able to inscribe themselves into their pictures — not just figuratively, but also literally, by means of more or less hidden signatures. This form of artistic autonomy was still new territory in Castiglione's time. And to this day, it is the technique of the monotype, however marginal it may initially appear in the artist's overall oeuvre, that offers the richest insights into this pioneering aspect of the Genoese artist.

Dedicated to the memory of my mother Christiane von Götz (1959–2021).

1 Tanner 2015, pp. 10–15. **2** Exh. cat. Cologne 2014. **3** Monotypes by Castiglione's contemporary Anthonis Sallaert have also come down to us. However, whether they preceded Castiglione's — as Martin Royalton-Kisch has suggested — must remain debatable in view of their uncertain dating. See Royalton-Kisch 1988, pp. 60–61. **4** Beyer 2010, pp. 189–203. **5** Exh. cat. Munich 2004, p. 14. **6** See more recently, exh. cat. London/Denver/Fort Worth 2013, p. 57. **7** It seems probable that the female bust was modelled after the so-called Madama Lucrezia, one of the "talking statues" of Rome. Ibid., p. 65. **8** It is evidently based on Gorgoneia such as the *Medusa Rondanini* with knots of snakes under the chin and wings on the head. **9** This was pointed out by Suhr 2010, p. 553. **10** Ibid., p. 552. **11** Exh. cat. Dresden 2019, p. 95. **12** Busch 1986, p. 49. **13** Calabi 1925, p. 226. **14** I am thinking here of cat. 70 and the corresponding monotype (TIB 4602.121). **15** Miller 1994, p. 66; see also Anita V. Sganzerla's essay in this volume, pp. 35–43. **16** On the contemplation of sculptures by torchlight as a form of social entertainment that had grown out of a studio practice among sixteenth-century artists, see Bätschmann 1997, pp. 21–22. **17** Welsh Reed 1991, p. 73. On this monotype, see also Standring 2012, pp. 172–173. **18** Exh. cat. New York 1980. **19** See more recently, Jeutter 2004, pp. 275–300. **20** Busch 1986, p. 55. **21** The provenance of the monotype now in Windsor can be traced back to Sagredo. On Sagredo and Castiglione's influence on Tiepolo, see the concise description of Haskell 1963, pp. 266–267.

Nature, Antiquity, and Philosophy in the Art of Castiglione

Anita V. Sganzerla

The philosophical background of Giovanni Benedetto Castiglione's art has long attracted scholarly interest. Attempts at uncovering the intellectual underpinning of the artist's intriguing inventions have been numerous. In particular, special emphasis has been placed on the investigation of the artist's cultural milieu in both Genoa and Rome, the intellectual interests of his patrons and fellow artists, and the probable literary sources for his iconographies. While some studies attempt a holistic approach, others center on specific paintings or small groups of related works. In Castiglione's oeuvre we regularly encounter the same subject matter being dealt with in different media, usually with distinct results in terms of iconography and thematic focus. Illuminating instances of this aspect of his practice are his novel treatments of *Temporalis Aeternitas* (cat. 66), *Diogenes Searching for an Honest Man* (cat. 65), and *Circe with the Companions of Odysseus Transformed into Animals* (cats. 27, 68), all centered on the themes of human nature, time, and vanitas.

While the extent of Castiglione's philosophical knowledge is destined to remain debatable, an important resource for the study of his art comes in the form of an archival record: the inventory of the library of his first master, the aristocratic artist Giovanni Battista Paggi.[1] While training with Paggi in circa 1625–1627, Castiglione would have had access to his master's collection of books, alongside the art objects and prints kept in his studio. Paggi's substantial

library, two-hundred-strong, was made up primarily of the staple texts for artists at the start of the seventeenth century: iconographic manuals, volumes on ancient history, and illustrated emblem compendiums, such as Cesare Ripa's *Iconologia* (Padua, 1603) and Vincenzo Cartari's *Imagini de gli dei* (Venice, 1556). In addition, Paggi put together a group of seventeen titles relating to fields of human knowledge not directly associated to the visual arts and covering such areas as natural philosophy, alchemy, magic, and hermetic knowledge. These included undescribed editions of, for instance, Giovanni Battista Della Porta's *Magia Naturalis* (probably the 1611 vulgate translation published in Naples), Giovan Battista Nazari's *Della Tramutatione Metallica Sogni Tre* (Brescia, 1572), and the Greek *Corpus Hermeticum*, the starting point for Hermeticism, translated into Latin by the Renaissance scholar Marsilio Ficino and first printed in Treviso in 1471.[2] Such readings were part of Paggi's intellectual edification and did not noticeably shape the contents of his art, but in the hands of the young and ambitious Castiglione they may have set him on a life-long personal quest. While Paggi's influence on the Genoese artistic debate of his time has long been acknowledged, the contents of his library have recently been the subject of renewed scholarly attention aimed at showing how the ideas contained in the treatises by Della Porta, Nazari, and others may have inspired Castiglione with the determination to imbue his artistic

Fig. 1
Giovanni Benedetto Castiglione
A Sorceress (Circe)
ca. 1651 · oil on canvas · 99 × 141 cm
Museo Poldi Pezzoli, Milan

practice and self-expression with philosophical depth when forging his artistic career in Rome.[3]

Such early ambitions allow us to trace a more nuanced profile of an artist who initially followed the tradition of his native Genoa by specializing in the naturalistic representation of animals. His skills in depicting all sorts of animals, in his biblical, pastoral, and mythological landscapes, would remain a trademark of Castiglione's art throughout his life, also influencing many of the artists who came into contact with his work. Soon departing from the significant examples of Giovanni Andrea de Ferrari, Sinibaldo Scorza, and the Flemish painters active in Genoa, Castiglione diversified his use of animal imagery. His preference for mythological and allegorical subjects that called for the inclusion of natural elements as bearers of new meaning greatly contributed to the originality of his artistic production. This is evinced in his many depictions of *Circe with the Companions of Odysseus Transformed into Animals* (cats. 27, 68), where the sorceress is shown in a detached or pensive pose, surrounded by a variety of animals and an array of objects alluding to the vanity of human ambitions (fig. 1). In line with the contemporary interest in reading myths as disguised moral lessons applicable to everyday life, Castiglione exploited the allusive nature of Circe's magic to deal with matters of morality, ethics, and human nature.[4] As we shall see, the human condition and its inherent conflicts preoccupied Castiglione throughout his life, in conjunction with his meditation on the passing of time and of man's place within history.

Fig. 2
Nicolas Poussin
Arcadian Shepherds
ca. 1629–1630 · oil on canvas · 101 × 82 cm
The Devonshire Collections

Fig. 3
Giovanni Benedetto Castiglione
Arcadian Shepherds
ca. 1655 · oil on canvas · 110.5 × 109.5 cm
The J. Paul Getty Museum, Malibu

Lessons from Antiquity

The turn of the seventeenth century marked a particularly poignant time for the reassessment of the historical and moral legacy of Classical Antiquity. And what better place for this discourse to unfold than Rome, the Holy City, literally built upon the vestiges of its past. During his early years in Rome (ca. 1632–1637), Castiglione came in contact with artists, men of letters, and collectors engaged in shaping a new artistic and cultural scenario. To make his debut on Rome's artistic stage he could rely on his ties to Genoese artists and patrons, as well as to prominent intellectuals who had links to his native city. These included the Sarzanese writer and intellectual Agostino Mascardi, active in the Barberini court, and author of *Dell'Arte Historica* (Rome, 1636).[5]

First posited by Francis Haskell, recent studies have mapped Castiglione's network in Barberini Rome and his association with the learned circle of the scholar and patron Cassiano dal Pozzo and his friend and protégé Nicolas Poussin.[6] With his extensive commissioning of drawings of antiquities for his *Museo Cartaceo*, Cassiano contributed greatly to charting Rome's ancient history through the testimony of its monuments. Moreover, he was directly involved with the posthumous publication of Antonio

Bosio's *Roma Sotterranea* (Rome, 1634).[7] This study of the recently rediscovered catacombs, believed to have been the setting for the liturgical life and martyrdom of the early Christians, sought to retrieve their memory from relics, artifacts, inscriptions, and epitaphs.

Already identified as a likely source for Castiglione's etching *The Finding of the Bodies of Saints Peter and Paul* (cat. 70), the material of *Roma Sotterranea*, together with the antiquarian and erudite interests of this milieu, seem to have inspired the Genoese artist more broadly. An early instance is given by the etching *Temporalis Aeternitas* (cat. 66).[8] This enigmatic allegory takes its initial inspiration from Poussin's *Arcadian Shepherds*, also referred to as *Et in Arcadia Ego*, two versions of which exist, now in Chatsworth House (fig. 2) and the Musée du Louvre respectively.[9] To convey a sense of mystery, Castiglione experimented with his evocative chiaroscuro, inspired by Rembrandt's night scenes, through which Poussin's elegiac realization of human destiny becomes an obscure revelation. The etching presents a torch-lit view of an ancient burial ground with five figures discovering an inscription on a tombstone, "TEMPORALIS AETERNITAS 1645." The central theme of time's inexorable passing, indicated by the crumbling stone of the tombs, funerary monuments, and epitaph, is combined with a meditation on the value of memory and the preservation of the past.[10] The two central figures sitting on the ground are intent on reading out and writing down the content of the inscription. Their proximity and similarity suggest a link with symbolic representations of memory, personified in Ripa's *Iconologia* as a woman with two faces holding a quill in her right hand and a book in her left.[11]

The theme of writing is further evoked in the presence of two inscriptions and in their materiality: one has been etched on the surface of the tombstone, to recall a carved epitaph, and the other engraved. Both inscriptions complicate the meaning of the print and have been the object of scholarly inquiry. "Temporalis Aeternitas" could mean that even eternity is temporal as it is made up of timebound moments, while the engraved quote "Nec sepulchra legens vereor ne perdam memoriam" is a reprise from a passage in Cicero's *Cato Maior de Senectute* (*Cato the Elder: On Old Age*). Countering an old superstition that reading epitaphs could affect one's mnemonic faculties, the antiquarian Cato claims that by reading epitaphs he is not weakening but in fact strengthening his memory by exercising it in recalling the dead.[12] This erudite quote was added by the print's publisher, Giovanni Domenico de Rossi, perhaps wishing to elucidate its meaning. When returning to the subject a decade later, Castiglione revisited the solemn mood of his early etching while still maintaining a sense of mystery. In the octagonal painting now in the J. Paul Getty Museum, Malibu, the discovery in a mysterious and ominous landscape of the same Latin motto on a tombstone startles a pair of shepherd-philosophers (fig. 3).[13]

In deciphering the imagery of *Temporalis Aeternitas* and reading the inscriptions, the beholder is actively engaged in uncovering its meaning, thus mirroring the actions of the protagonists of the scene. Through their very making, Castiglione's works call for the kind of attentive scrutiny capable of triggering a deeper meditation on their meaning. Whether dealing with scenes of solemn revelation or miraculous subjects, through his mastery of light and darkness in his etchings and monotypes, the artist thematized the acts of looking, discovering, and unveiling, as further attested by his most "philosophical" inventions.

The Philosopher's Quest

In the seventeenth century the portrayal of ancient philosophers and of exemplary anecdotes from their lives flourished, thanks in part to a re-evaluation of their legacy.[14] The fascination with the teachings of the Cynics and Stoics is revealed, for instance, in the Jesuit Daniello Bartoli's *L'uomo di lettere difeso ed emendato* (Rome, 1645), where the ancient philosophers are held up as examples of virtue.

Castiglione's etching *Diogenes Searching for an Honest Man* (cat. 65) is freely inspired by an anecdote from the *Lives and Opinions of Eminent Philosophers* by the biographer of the Greek philosophers, Diogenes Laertius (*fl.* ca. third century AD).[15] Diogenes the Cynic would wander the streets in broad daylight holding a lit candle, saying that he was looking for a man.[16] The philosopher was looking for a man who lived self-sufficiently and in accordance with nature,

Fig. 4
Giovanni Benedetto Castiglione
Diogenes Searching for a Man
ca. 1640–1645 · oil on canvas · 97 × 145 cm
Museo Nacional del Prado, Madrid

Fig. 5

Salvator Rosa

Diogenes and Alexander

1661–1662 · etching and drypoint · plate: 45.2 × 27 cm

Harvard Art Museums/Fogg Museum

a man who was aware of the low value of earthly possessions and artificial structures imposed by society, and his critique of man was to inspire countless reflections on the role of the wise individual within society. In Castiglione's etching, the philosopher's quest takes him to a ruined landscape where he finds, not men, but animals, which may symbolize human baseness (the owl of superstition, the monkey of imitation and wickedness, and the tortoise of sloth). However, the emphasis on nature and the primitive state of man (primeval landscape, wild plants, animals, skull, pagan artifacts) both in the etching and in the painting now in the Museo Nacional del Prado, may instead be a reminder of the necessity to study and comprehend nature, the primary model and teacher for the philosopher but also for the artist (fig. 4).[17] Both works, with their multiple references to the curiosities of nature and art, and the language of symbols, evoke the collecting interests of Rome's intellectual circles, in particular the entourage of Cassiano dal Pozzo and the Accademia dei Lincei, the scientific academy named after the sharp-eyed lynx. As Helen Langdon has observed, Castiglione's etching is "redolent of the atmosphere of scientific Rome in the middle years of the century, when Galileo had been condemned, and there was now a renewed interest in magic and alchemy side by side with modern experimental science."[18] Simultaneously, Castiglione's works are pervaded by a sense of decay and decadence, open to different interpretations. This is corroborated, for instance, by the lascivious figure of the reclining satyr (or Pan) in the Madrid painting, whose head is juxtaposed to that of the goat, as if to emphasize his animalistic side, in what appears to me to be a nod to Giovanni Battista Della Porta's influential treatise on human and animal physiognomy, *De Humana Physiognomonia* (Sorrento, 1586).[19] Most scholars have interpreted the figure as standing for baseness, while a recent reading has connected it, and indeed the painting's composition as a whole, to a preferable, more natural condition, from a long-lost time when man lived in concord with his instincts.[20]

Contemporary readers were fascinated by Diogenes' independence and praise of nature's simplicity: he lived in a barrel and was said to envy the snail's ability to always carry its house on its back — which may explain the small snail in the foreground of Castiglione's print. His self-sufficiency made him impervious to the flattery of the rich and powerful, as best demonstrated by the famous episode of his encounter with Alexander the Great, painted and etched by Salvator Rosa (fig. 5).[21] While Renaissance rulers, identifying with Alexander, used the story to cast themselves as enlightened protectors of art and philosophy, in the period

Fig. 6
Giovanni Benedetto Castiglione
Melancholy
ca. 1645–1646 · etching · plate: 21.7 × 11.4 cm
Harvard Art Museums/Fogg Museum

under scrutiny here it was more often read as a commentary on the perils encountered by the wise man, the modern-day equivalent of Diogenes, negotiating his place within court culture.

The story of Alexander's visit to Diogenes, as recounted by Plutarch in his *Lives of the Noble Greeks and Romans*, tells of the mighty ruler visiting the philosopher one day and asking whether there was anything he wished for.[22] To which Diogenes replied that all he desired was for Alexander to move out of the sun and stop casting a shadow on him, as it was depriving him of the one thing not in his power to give. These words aroused the admiration of Alexander, who understood the true nature of Diogenes' state of freedom and happiness. Although his men were struck by the philosopher's insolence, the ruler commented that, had he not been Alexander, he would have wanted to be Diogenes. The anecdote, which highlights Diogenes' intransigence and intellectual independence, is recalled in the dedicatory lines added to Castiglione's print by its publisher ("he could with such severity decline the favors of Alexander"). Giovanni Domenico de Rossi's chosen dedicatee was the Roman collector and connoisseur Nicolò Simonelli, who was a friend and patron of Rosa, Pietro Testa, and Pier Francesco Mola, all well known for their treatment of philosophical themes.[23] These artists' choice of subject matter and their conscious decision to associate their names with those of the ancient philosophers beg the question: did they also wish to be likened to virtuous men, untainted by base ambitions and man's insatiable thirst for wealth?

The Painter-Philosopher

Because of his moralizing subjects, his frequent allusions to the theme of vanitas, and a seemingly pessimistic view of human nature, Castiglione is one of a group of seventeenth-century artists often referred to as painter-philosophers. Rosa, who identified with the irreverent Diogenes, was even celebrated as "pittore filosofo" by his fellow academicians at the Accademia dei Percossi in Florence.[24] Testa's art and theoretical writings, meanwhile, express his profound admiration for Platonic philosophy and especially for the figure of Socrates.[25] By critiquing contemporary customs and upholding the lives of the Cynics and Stoics as virtuous examples, these artists carved out a distinctive identity for themselves. Distinguishing between their moral conduct, their aspirations, and their artistic "disguise" is often difficult. If they shared their contemporaries' concerns regarding the role of the intellectual within the deceitful realm of court culture – rife with ambition, envy, and scheming – they were also all too aware of the necessity to "play the game" to secure commissions and support their social standing.[26] By supplying private patrons and the print market with suggestive depictions of philosophical subjects or moralizing tales, these artists were demonstrating their intellectual sympathies as much as their professional shrewdness. The same artists who celebrated the Greek philosophers as outsiders by painting them in tattered clothes and who made constant reference to the futility of human ambitions had no qualms trumpeting their own fertile imagination and powers of invention, as exemplified by the

Fig. 7
Salvator Rosa
Democritus in Meditation
1650–1651 · oil on canvas · 344 × 214 cm
Statens Museum for Kunst, Copenhagen

extravagant print *The Genius of Castiglione* (before 1648; cat. 67).[27] In Rosa's version of the subject (1660–1665), inspired by Castiglione's precedent, the youthful genius wears an ivy crown, sacred to Bacchus, to signify the "inspired and mysterious qualities" of the artist's own genius, while the upended cornucopia spills coins and jewels signaling his disdain of material wealth.[28] Through their choice of subjects and their ambivalent relationship with fame and fortune, these artists affirmed themselves as original witnesses to and, moreover, protagonists in the learned debates of their time.[29]

A final example from Castiglione's etched oeuvre will cast further light on the convergence of moral philosophy, antiquity, and nature in his art: *Melancholy* (fig. 6). In it, a woman sits on the ground surrounded by the vestiges of the past overgrown with wild vegetation. In her lap she holds a skull and a musical score. Her absorbed pose recalls that of the eponymous figure in Albrecht Dürer's *Melencolia I* (1514), while other references to the state of the melancholic are also present. The cat and dog with their tense bodies allude to folly, the state of fluctuation between excitement and depression caused by melancholy. Scattered on the ground lie the instruments of human activity and ambition, both scientific (compasses and square) and intellectual-artistic (palette and brushes, book, sheet music, and lute). An armillary sphere and a scroll rest next to the figure. The discarded objects on the ground are presented as if to signify the futility of those same worldly endeavors they stand for. Moreover, as in the case of *Temporalis Aeternitas*, the publisher, perhaps wishing to complement the meaning of the image, inscribed it with the words "Ubi Inletabilitas ibi Virtus," typically interpreted in a neo-Stoic vein as "Virtue lies where there is imperviousness to joy."[30] While the original meaning of the motto is a matter of speculation, the potential of Castiglione's inventions rests precisely on the way they stimulate discussion around multifaceted matters of universal scope.

Melancholy and Castiglione's other prints of moral subjects were sources of great inspiration for Rosa in the 1650s, as attested by his ambitious painting, *Democritus in Meditation*, in the Statens Museum for Kunst, Copenhagen (fig. 7).[31] Here the solitary philosopher is seen contemplating the futility of intellectual endeavors. Besides referring to vanitas, the decaying monuments, skulls, skeletons, and dead animals in the foreground also refer to the scientific debates of the time, and to the antiquarian and collecting habits that prevailed in Rome's erudite circles, as exemplified by the famous collection of the Jesuit polymath Athanasius Kircher.[32] The vanity of knowledge and ultimately of human life itself is at the center of Rosa's *Moral Philosophy* (ca. 1649–1650), where the female personification of the discipline, presented with her arm resting on a skull, shows Rosa looking once again at Dürer's and Castiglione's melancholic figures.[33]

If, for Rosa, the melancholic pose became that of the moral philosopher conscious of the futility of all things, for Castiglione that meditation continued in some of his depictions of Circe (see fig. 1). Indeed, Circe's power to alter men's appearance by transforming them into animals, coupled with her ability to corrupt, lent itself to an array of metaphorical interpretations. Is Circe's melancholy caused by the realization of men's true nature? The value of these

associations lives on and resurfaces in the words of Castiglione's younger brother and follower, Salvatore. In a letter, written in 1662 to their mutual patron in Mantua, Duke Carlo II Gonzaga, Salvatore relies on a common trope regarding the perils of life at court by stating that he will not let himself be dragged down by the damned vice of loathsome ambition that would otherwise expose him to "the metamorphosis."[34] Salvatore's words seem to echo the allusive imagery and moralizing tone of Giovanni Benedetto's inventions.

1 Leonardi 2013, pp. 207–229. **2** Montanari 2020, pp. 6, 10–12. **3** Ibid.; Magnani 2014. **4** See, e.g., Ciliberto 2004; Frascarelli 2016, pp. 127–138. **5** Magnani 2014, pp. 215–234. **6** Haskell 1963, p. 114; exh. cat. Philadelphia 1971, p. 26; Di Penta 2014; see also Santucci 1985. **7** Herklotz 1992, pp. 31–38. **8** See exh. cat. Genoa 1990, cat. 61. **9** Blunt 1966, cats. 119–120. **10** Sganzerla 2017. **11** Ripa 1630, part 2, p. 464. **12** Davis 1958, p. 169; exh. cat. Philadelphia 1971, cat. E13. **13** See exh. cat. Genoa 1990, cat. 26; cf. Frascarelli 2016, pp. 199–206. **14** See Ferrari 1986. **15** Exh. cat. Genoa 1990, cat. 63. **16** Laertius 1853, p. 231. **17** Montanari 2020, p. 29; exh. cat. Washington 2020, cat. 43. **18** Langdon 2007, p. 173. **19** See Della Porta 1627, pp. 64, 119. **20** Frascarelli 2016, p. 73. **21** Wallace 1979, cat. 108; Volpi 2014, cat. 96. **22** Plutarch 1914–1926, vol. 7, 1919, p. 259. **23** Albl 2014. **24** See Volpi 2010. **25** Albl/Canevari 2014. **26** See, e.g., Snyder 2009. **27** Exh. cat. London/Denver/Fort Worth 2013, pp. 63, 67. **28** Wallace 1965, p. 480. **29** See Salerno 1970. **30** Exh. cat. Philadelphia 1971, cat. E14; Bernheimer 1951, p. 50. **31** Volpi 2014, cat. 162. **32** See, e.g., Findlen 2004. **33** Private collection; Volpi 2014, cat. 159. **34** Quoted in Meroni 1971, p. 78.

Rembrandt: An Early and a Late Source of Influence for Castiglione

Nadine M. Orenstein

Castiglione began etching during a period of effervescent creativity in the art of printmaking throughout Europe. During this time, the medium, with its own language of line and tone, was experimented with and pushed in inventive ways to respond to ever greater flights of Baroque expressiveness. While artists like Peter Paul Rubens viewed printmaking and its ability to reproduce a single image over potentially hundreds or even thousands of impressions as a means of publicizing his painted images and sharing them with a broad audience, others approached it as an artistic medium in its own right. They created work that paralleled or even differed greatly from what they produced on canvas. They went beyond the mere printing of etched black lines of ink on white paper and examined ways in which variations in strokes, inking, and paper tone might be called upon as the means for developing virtuosic works of art to be appreciated for their own sake. Federico Barocci and Jacques Bellange communicated the texture of skin through passages of soft stippling. Jacques Callot developed a tool called the *échoppe*, that imitated the swelling lines of engraving in the technique of etching. Hercules Segers invented soft-ground etching and produced highly original colored landscape "paintings" by printing on colored papers and hand-coloring prints. Castiglione's highly original monotypes, which occupy a space somewhere between drawing and print, can also be counted among the remarkable technical innovations in the medium conceived in this moment in art history.

Castiglione, a passionate printmaker, must have studied the work of such contemporaries and more, but it was the work of the Dutch printmaker Rembrandt van Rijn, whose career-long exploration of how a black-and-white medium might produce richly tonal images evocative of the effects achievable in painting, which captivated the Italian above all. Rembrandt's work struck a chord and the artist repeatedly returned to the Dutchman's figure types, compositions, and handling of line and tone. Castiglione may have recognized in Rembrandt a kindred spirit. In order to achieve their vision, both artists stretched the limitations of traditional media and rethought the ways in which they could exploit printmaking tools, ink, and the handling of line. This essay will examine Castiglione's evolving relationship with Rembrandt's work and what the Italian took away from the work of his northern counterpart.

Castiglione and Rembrandt were contemporaries, the Dutchman merely three years older than the Italian. Rembrandt began making etchings around 1625 but his investigations into the possibilities printmaking could offer began in earnest around 1628–1630. Castiglione's earliest prints are thought to date not too long after that, in the mid-1630s. Among the many prints that Rembrandt created during his early period were numerous small etchings of heads depicting himself and figures around him that were in essence studies of expression. Castiglione must certainly have seen a few of these. For example, the rare head of a man shouting (*Oriental Wearing a Headdress*)[1] seems to have been inspired by such small etchings by Rembrandt as *Self-Portrait Open-Mouthed As If Shouting* (1630).[2] Castiglione was clearly fascinated by this sort of *tronie*, a typically Dutch

Fig. 1
Rembrandt van Rijn
Self-Portrait Leaning on a Stone Sill
1639 · etching and drypoint
plate: 20 × 16 cm
The Metropolitan Museum of Art, New York

genre of small painting or print which can be defined as a study in expression or character of a figure sometimes dressed in unusual costume. Castiglione responded to this genre in his series of *Large* and *Small Oriental Heads* (cats. 58–63).

Determining when Castiglione first took note of Rembrandt's work can be complicated because much of the Italian artist's work is not dated. *Flock of Sheep Surrounding a Laden Donkey*,[3] generally dated by scholars to circa 1638–1640, seems to show early signs of Castiglione having a close look at Rembrandt's prints. In contrast to other bright and open works generally dated to slightly earlier, here Castiglione communicated a range of chiaroscuro tones by building layers of broad hatching added one over another through repeated bitings of the copperplate. This type of layering of varied hatching is a hallmark of Rembrandt's etching style and something that Castiglione adopted and made his own. Later works like *The Entry of the Animals into the Ark* (cat. 73) and *Circe with the Companions of Odysseus Transformed into Animals* (cat. 68) show the artist's later iteration of this style, whereby foliage and dark shadow are created with dense networks of straight lines, squiggles, short dashes, and dots.

Evidence of Castiglione's direct study of Rembrandt's prints can be found among his drawings. Several surviving sketches show that the artist copied details directly from prints by the Dutch master. For instance, the pen-and-ink sheet *Studies of Heads* (mid- to late 1630s),[4] shows the artist looking closely at Rembrandt and adapting and inventing Rembrandtesque character types. These types, replete with turbans and full beards, appear repeatedly throughout his work as, for instance, in the drawing *David before Saul* (cat. 42), an Old Testament subject treated many times by Rembrandt and his pupils.

Castiglione was clearly impressed by the way that Rembrandt applied lines in print and he carefully studied the northern artist's handling and devised his own response to it. The mix of tight zigzags with short flicks overlayed with long straight hatchings can be found, for instance, in Castiglione's *A Presumed Self-Portrait* (cat. 55) on the hat, the hair, and shoulder. The mustachioed figure with his tilted cap, long locks, and direct gaze toward the viewer is a clear nod to Rembrandt's 1639 *Self-Portrait Leaning on a Stone Sill* (fig. 1). In the self-portrait, the fabric of the coat displays Rembrandt's dense layering to reveal patterns, folds, and highlights, and Castiglione echoes this technique in the shadowed areas of the hair around the cheeks and chin. Lines on the lower right side of Castiglione's figure briefly indicate the shoulder and back. They suggest that, had more of the figure been etched, it would have been posed simi-

Fig. 2
Jan Lievens
Bust of an Old Man with a Fur Collar
1630–1640 · etching · plate: 16.2 × 14.5 cm
The Metropolitan Museum of Art, New York

larly to that in Rembrandt's self-portrait, with the shoulder and arm turned parallel to the picture plane. Castiglione may have run into problems that prevented the lines at the bottom from etching into the printing plate, or it could be that he intentionally blocked out the lower section of the print before etching the plate. In any event, he seems to have been satisfied with the result, which, in contrast to the Rembrandt, places the focus entirely on the face and the arresting stare of the sitter. Rembrandt based his self-portrait on Raphael's painted *Portrait of Baldassare Castiglione* (ca. 1514–1515),[5] which the artist sketched at the time it came up for auction in Amsterdam in 1639.[6] One wonders whether Giovanni Benedetto Castiglione was aware of this connection with this similarly named predecessor.

When discussing how Castiglione looked to the works of Rembrandt, we must clarify that we are in fact talking about a cluster of works by and after Rembrandt and by artists in his circle. This becomes most clear when examining his sources for the group of *Large Oriental Heads* (cats. 58–62), the set of five etchings of male heads, shown mostly in profile or three-quarter view, that are encircled by sweeping lines of hatching combined with shorter zigzagging lines. The artist was no doubt familiar with Rembrandt's

Fig. 3
Rembrandt van Rijn
The Raising of Lazarus: The Larger Plate
ca. 1632 · etching and engraving
plate: 36.6 × 25.8 cm
Rijksmuseum, Amsterdam

Four Oriental Heads,[7] etched in 1635. But Rembrandt himself had copied and adapted these from an earlier series by Jan Lievens. In the 1620s the two young Dutchmen worked together in Leiden and shared a studio, models, and a style. *Man with a Beard and Mustache, Wearing a Tasseled Head-dress, Facing Left* (cat. 60) comes very close in detail to an etched head of similar size by Lievens, *Bust of an Old Man with a Fur Collar* (fig. 2).[8] The profile of the bushy-browed faces with their broad, sloped noses and tight, pouting mouths are almost identical. The prints are in reverse to each other and that is not surprising. Castiglione would have copied or even traced the figure onto the printing plate in the same direction as the original, and, as a result of the reversal that occurs during the printing process, its head would face the opposite direction in the final print on paper. It has been rightly suggested that a source for Castiglione's *Bearded Old Man with His Head Leaning Forward* (cat. 61) is the print by Jan van Vliet after Rembrandt, *Bust of an Old Man with a Beard and Cap* (1634).[9] Van Vliet was engaged by Rembrandt in the early 1630s to make a number of such prints after his paintings. On the other hand, *Man Wearing a Plumed Fur Cap and a Scarf* (cat. 62) from this group seems to derive quite directly from a work by Rembrandt, his *Self-Portrait in a Cap and Scarf with the Face Dark* (1633; cat. 56), not only in the highly shadowed face of the figure but even the scarf loosely draped around his neck. While drawing inspiration from Rembrandt here, Castiglione notably took an opposite approach to depicting a face entirely in shadow. While Rembrandt cast his own face in deep shadow, he left touches of light on the nose, eyes, cheek, and chin that give it a sense of three-dimensionality. He understood that within a darkened image, highlights can bring out shapes. Castiglione followed a different tack: he deepened the darkest shadows as well as the eyes, introducing no specific highlights to the face. This forced the linework alone to communicate a sense of three-dimensionality. While taking his own approach, it is clear that Castiglione carefully studied a range of images by Rembrandt's circle, examining not only their subjects but also how line was applied and shadow constructed. Rather than merely referencing a single sheet, he examined a body of works and synthesized the lessons learned for his own purposes.

How, then, did Castiglione get to see the works of these Netherlandish artists? The most likely source would have been the Flemish artist-dealer Cornelis de Wael who was based in Genoa. He and his brother Lucas traveled from Antwerp to Italy in 1619. Cornelis established himself in Genoa and remained there while his brother Lucas returned home in 1628. De Wael, who made a number of etchings himself,

Fig. 4
Rembrandt van Rijn
Christ Crucified between the Two Thieves: The Three Crosses
1653 · drypoint · plate: 38.1 × 43.8 cm
The Metropolitan Museum of Art, New York

is known to have sold a variety of works, among them prints by Rembrandt. The inventory of his estate, compiled in 1667, lists 134 prints by Rembrandt which appear to have been items for sale rather than studio material.[10] The prints were assembled in albums, portfolios of loose prints, and small booklets. It seems clear that by the mid-1640s, Castiglione had at his disposal a collection, possibly an album, of early works by Rembrandt, Lievens, and van Vliet, which he consulted as sources of inspiration.

In general, scholars have viewed the period of Castiglione's deepest engagement with Rembrandt as falling roughly between 1645 to 1650, a time that coincides with the artist's activity first in Genoa and then in Rome, after he abruptly left his native city in 1647. He returned to Genoa again in 1652. The artist appears to have brought his printing plates with him to Rome since several prints were republished there by Giovanni Giacomo de Rossi in 1648. One of these works was *Temporalis Aeternitas* (cat. 66) which was created in 1645, the date inscribed on the tomb at the left, but many of the known impressions also bear De Rossi's publisher's address and the later date. In the etching, a bright flaming torch illuminates the scene, whose subject of death and the transitory nature of earthly accomplishments must have been inspired by Poussin.[11] Although the print is less overtly Rembrandtesque than others discussed above, a recognized source of inspiration for the work was an etching by

Fig. 5
Rembrandt van Rijn
The Entombment
ca. 1654 · etching and drypoint
plate: 21.1 × 16 cm
The Metropolitan Museum of Art, New York

Rembrandt, *The Raising of Lazarus: The Larger Plate* (ca. 1632; fig. 3).[12] In the Rembrandt, Christ, depicted from the side, his back in shadow, stands over the brightly illuminated scene of Lazarus rising from his tomb. The source of the illumination is not visible but appears to emanate from the right. The composition of the Castiglione reverses in a general sense that of the Rembrandt, even in the way that the light enters from one side. A draped man with a beard is depicted from the side, his back in shadow, echoing Rembrandt's Christ. He looks down toward the brightly lit ground below while the scene is lit by a large torch on the left. With the still life consisting of a turban, a sword, and other arms, Castiglione acknowledged his source in the Rembrandt where a similar still life hangs at the top center. In this print and the related *Theseus Finding His Father's Weapons* (1645),[13] Castiglione defined forms with the now-familiar layers of lines, long hatching, and short zigzags. He further employed dotted patterns to express a light shadow on the skin. Castiglione generously applied such stippling in the later version of *Temporalis Aeternitas* (1655).[14]

Castiglione's interest in Rembrandt culminated in a group of three similarly rich tenebrist biblical subjects that he must have executed in close succession, *Tobit Burying the Dead* (cat. 69), *The Finding of the Bodies of Saints Peter and Paul* (cat. 70), and *The Raising of Lazarus* (cat. 71). In these outstanding examples of printmaking, Castiglione mastered and assimilated the lessons of chiaroscuro and technical innovation that he had mined from the works of his counterpart in the north. In a recent PhD dissertation on the artist, Alexandra Blanc studied the artist's complex working method in *The Raising of Lazarus*, analyzing how he densely worked the copperplate over a series of states.[15] Not only did he build up the depth of the shadows with many layers of etching but he also scraped away and burnished the copperplate to produce a range of highlights. He began with a gray base-tone, created from the unburnished copperplate, densely covered with scratches. From there, he employed diverse tools and lines – both adding and eliminating ones – to create the rich, dark, and contrasting lighter shades as well as the bright whites that surround Christ.[16] As in the works discussed above, references to Rembrandt's early prints can be found among the figures in all three etchings. For instance, in *Tobit Burying the Dead*, while the classical ruins and sculpture in the background make reference to the artist's Poussiniste inspiration, the bearded Tobit, with his bent cap and bowed pose, and his dog busy surveying the scene on the left are truly Rembrandtesque. Indeed, the hunched Tobit seems to derive from Rembrandt's early etchings of beggars.[17]

Scholars have often dated the group of three prints to the period between 1647–1651 when Castiglione was active in Rome.[18] Castiglione would have been in contact with De Rossi and other printmakers there and it seems likely that his printmaking would have developed and flowered in that environment.[19] However, Blanc has made a case for moving the group somewhat earlier to 1645 or even before, when Castiglione was still living in Genoa. Her premise is based on the connection of Castiglione's *Raising of Lazarus* to his brother Salvatore's etching of the same subject securely dated to 1645; the theory being that Salavatore is unlikely to have attempted this image, highly inspired by Rembrandt, without his brother's precedent.[20] Like Giovanni Benedetto's work, Salvatore's print takes its inspiration from etchings by Rembrandt and Jan Lievens. While Blanc's thesis has some merit, we must consider the equal likelihood of a younger sibling producing something new, and thereby making the older sibling rethink what they had been doing. I would like to make a different case here, one that moves the dating of the works in the opposite direction, to a much later time than usually supposed, to the mid-

Fig. 6
Rembrandt van Rijn
The Adoration of the Shepherds: A Night Piece
ca. 1657 · etching, engraving, and drypoint
with plate tone · plate: 14.6 × 19.5 cm
The Metropolitan Museum of Art, New York

1650s, the period when Castiglione had once again returned to Genoa. At that time, Castiglione would have been exposed to a fresh group of works by Rembrandt: the artist's dark, richly inked late prints, which may have influenced the way Castiglione handled these tenebrist etchings.

A first observation to support a later dating is a purely visual one. The three prints of *Tobit Burying the Dead*, *The Finding of the Bodies of Saints Peter and Paul*, and *The Raising of Lazarus* show a deep understanding of the subtle ways in which light plays within a dark setting, one that is very different and much more sophisticated than the handling of chiaroscuro that we encounter in *Temporalis Aeternitas* and *Theseus Finding His Father's Weapons* of 1645. The differences suggest that the two groups of works date from different points in the artist's career. In *Temporalis Aeternitas* the torch is the single source of light and it brightly illuminates the center of the composition. Yet, Castiglione permeates the scene with light in such a way that makes it seem quite unlikely to be emanating from that specific source alone. In the *Theseus Finding His Father's Weapons*,

a large space is blazingly illuminated but, similarly, there is no directional indication among the highlights to suggest that their source is the torch. In the three biblical prints, however, Castiglione was much more thoughtful about the lighting and how the light from a torch might make its way onto surfaces within a darkened space. In *The Finding of the Bodies of Saints Peter and Paul*, the torch at the center casts light on the bodies' legs but notably leaves their torsos and heads, which are further away, in greater shade. The light touches the group of onlookers on the right. They are progressively plunged into shadow as they recede from the source. In addition, Castiglione created highlights on the outstanding elements of their faces; the noses and foreheads catch the light while other parts remain in shadow. Similarly, in *The Raising of Lazarus*, the most brightly lit parts of Lazarus are those closest to and facing the torch, while the group of onlookers on the right – most proximate to the torch – are illuminated even more brightly. Again the light dances across their faces, resting only upon certain features. For instance, a small

Fig. 7
Rembrandt van Rijn
Christ Appearing to the Apostles
1656 · etching · plate: 16.2 × 21 cm
Rijksmuseum, Amsterdam

bright touch highlights the nose of the man at the back of the group who, facing forward, is otherwise left completely shrouded in shadow. Here Castiglione incorporated something that Rembrandt also puzzled with throughout his career: the idea that to show something in the dark, you have to bring out the touches of light. We saw this already in Rembrandt's early *Self-Portrait in a Cap and Scarf with the Face Dark* (1633) but he continued to explore this puzzle in his etchings of the mid-1640s, for example in *The Portrait of Jan Six* (1647)[21] and *Self-Portrait Etching at a Window* (1648),[22] and even beyond that through the 1650s. It seems likely that Castiglione was carefully studying, just as he had in the past, how his northern counterpart handled this artistic challenge.

Potential sources for some of the figures and compositional elements in the three biblical prints point us further toward a conclusion that Castiglione must have consulted Rembrandt's etchings of the mid-1650s. In the right foreground of *Tobit Burying the Dead*, a woman walks away from the scene as she turns her head to glance at the grave nearby. The odd twisting of her upper body has been associated with a figure in the left background of Rembrandt's *Lazarus* (fig. 3), who is depicted waist-length and clasps his hands in one direction while looking in the other at the miracle taking place before him.[23] While that figure may have been a source, his hunched shoulders forming an arc behind his head differ from the manner in which Castiglione depicted his cloaked figure. Much closer to the figure in *Tobit Burying the Dead* is a similarly placed turbaned figure seen walking toward the right in the foreground of one of Rembrandt's most famous late prints, *Christ Crucified between the Two Thieves: The Three Crosses* (1653; fig. 4). The uncomfortably posed figure – lit from behind, squared shoulders facing right, tilting his head to the left while stepping with his left foot toward the right – is nearly identical in pose to Castiglione's woman. More generally, the composition of the *Three Crosses*, with its brightly lit central scene that partially illuminates the participants from differing angles in relation to their distance from the center, could well have inspired Castiglione's placement of the light at the center of *Tobit Burying the Dead*.

In composition, *The Finding of the Bodies of Saints Peter and Paul* seems to have been inspired by Rembrandt's *Entombment* (cat. 51), which is usually dated to around 1654. The vertical scene with the bodies laid out at the bottom and a group looking over the scene is a reversed arrangement to that of Rembrandt's *Entombment*. Both are lit by candlelight. The background in both images is comprised of an arched shape at the top and a horizontal ledge or wall in the center that divides the upper and lower halves of the composition. While the impression included in the catalog here is from the darkly inked second state when Rembrandt "painted" the printing plate in such a way as to highlight only certain aspects of the composition, some of the significant details are actually more visible in the cleanly wiped impressions of the first state (fig. 5). The triangularly clustered group of onlookers in both Castiglione's *The Finding of the Bodies of Saints Peter and Paul* and his *Raising of Lazarus* may have been inspired by a similarly constructed group in Rembrandt's *Adoration of the Shepherds: A Night Piece* (ca. 1657; fig. 6), one of the artist's darkest images, in which the shepherds, arriving to catch a glimpse of the Virgin and Child, emerge out of the gloom by way of the small touches of light on their faces and clothes.

Finally, Castiglione's treatment of the bright halo of light in *The Raising of Lazarus* may derive from a late print by Rembrandt, *Christ Appearing to the Apostles* (1656; fig. 7).[24] Castiglione ingeniously created the light around Christ's head with rays of broken lines, squiggles, and scratches, executed in several campaigns of work on the plate, involving different tools and techniques: etching and scratching, painting with stopping-out varnish, as well as scraping and burnishing the plate. The effect is one of darker and lighter lines encircling Christ's head, some of them seemingly disappearing and breaking into particles. Rembrandt did not work his plate as intensely but the final effect is similar; his Christ is surrounded by a burst of light that similarly breaks up and dissolves the surrounding etched rays. It seems likely that Castiglione knew of the Rembrandt as he created his own etching.

As he produced the three biblical prints, Castiglione seems to have consulted a wider range of works by Rembrandt than he had before: early works but also, strikingly, some from the mid-1650s. He had already in the 1640s demonstrated a fascination with creating chiaroscuro in print, when he made *Temporalis Aeternitas* and *Theseus Finding His Father's Weapons* as well as the early dark monotypes. By the mid-1650s, he was able to execute such chiaroscuro images in a more refined way. By that time, he had at his disposal later works by his northern contemporary that showed how Rembrandt, absorbed by similar artistic questions, had resolved them. And at that point, Castiglione himself was a more seasoned printmaker with more technical tricks up his sleeve, which we see him using to full advantage in *The Raising of Lazarus*.

Over his long printmaking career, Castiglione internalized the lessons that he drew from Rembrandt's work and came up with something of his own. Castiglione's great attention and repeated quotations from Rembrandt's oeuvre should not be viewed in a negative light. This was part of the artistic process at the time and Rembrandt himself repeatedly drew upon the work of numerous and wide-ranging artistic predecessors. Such sources allow us a glimpse into the artist's mind and, as a result, we can gain some insight into what interested him artistically when he looked at the work of others. Castiglione was clearly fascinated by how compositions were constructed, where figures should be positioned, how light illuminates space, and the types and specific combinations of lines that can be employed in an etching to express texture and shadow. He was clearly fascinated by how Rembrandt did things, and without the possibility of ever meeting the Dutchman (who famously refused to travel to Italy) for long discussions in person, Castiglione had to take a close, hard look at the prints and respond if not in words, then in lines.

1 TIB 4602.055. 2 NH I.67. 3 TIB 4602.029. 4 The Royal Collection / HM Queen Elizabeth II, Windsor Castle, RCIN 903944. 5 Musée du Louvre, Paris, inv. 61.1. 6 Albertina, Vienna, inv. 8859. 7 NH I.149–152. 8 Jeutter 2004, cats. 58, 59, pp. 280–281. 9 Ibid., cats. 56, 57 pp. 278–279. 10 Rutgers 2003, p. 13 and the document is included among the Rembrandt documents at http://remdoc.huygens.knaw.nl/#/document/remdoc/e13085. 11 Exh. cat. Philadelphia 1971, cat. E13 with further discussion of the subject. 12 Blanc 2017, pp. 46–47. 13 TIB 4602.024. 14 TIB 4602.027. 15 Blanc 2017, pp. 21–42. 16 Ibid., pp. 24–26. 17 For instance, *Beggar in a High Hat, Leaning on a Stick* (NH I.41). 18 See exh. cat. Philadelphia 1971, cats. E20–22. 19 Ibid., cat. E20. 20 Blanc 2017, p. 48. 21 NH II.238. 22 NH II.240. 23 Jeutter 2004, pp. 233, 272. 24 Another potential source might be Rembrandt's *Supper at Emmaus* (NH II.283).

Catalog

Drawings

Castiglione's drawings stand apart from those of his Italian seicento contemporaries largely because the bulk of his sheets are oil sketches on unprimed paper. Since many appear unfinished, they draw attention to his process of making them, which led Raffaele Soprani, his earliest biographer, to comment about the artist's brushwork as "grazioso, facile." Such traits call attention to Castiglione's distinctive *maniera* that informs virtually all of his works on paper. Because the medium *is* oil after all, painting on unprepared paper could be problematic. Too much oil would stain the paper, bleeding beyond the boundaries of the intended lines. Too little oil would result in dry mark-making lacking fluency of execution across the paper. Castiglione overcame such technical challenges by experimenting on sheet after sheet, and in doing so learned about the medium's capabilities and limitations and the mesmerizing properties of "painting on paper."

He also learned how to vary the pressure of his brush on the surface, how to modulate the transparency or opacity of his pigments, how to control the extent to which the oil stains bled into the paper as he drew, either by reducing the oil content of the medium or by adding small amounts of lead white in order to lessen the time the oils took to dry. All of these factors would determine whether he would be left with a field of extensive oil stains on the paper or more solid forms painted with semi-dry pigments. This gave a deliberate contrast between broader, paler, more diffuse background areas of pigment, and darker, sharper passages to pick out details and increase the illusion of volume (echoing the practice of drawing with a quill or reed pen and then adding patches of wash).

Most often, by restricting his palette to a narrow range of earth pigments, Castiglione was able to concentrate on tonal effects without having to take account of color while at the same time never appearing monochromatic. And, as we can see in a number of drawings here, he also discovered that additional touches of color, adroitly placed, could elevate a good drawing into a brilliant one. His brush drawings become more complicated when he introduces additional colors.

What makes Castiglione's drawings so special is that they were conceived as finished works of art, despite their deliberately *non-finito* (unfinished) appearance. Some may have been made for sale, others for personal use in the studio, perhaps as models for a growing repertoire of subjects or to instruct his assistants. The fact that so many of his drawings survive demonstrates that he (and others) cherished them. But the paucity of drawings as preliminary sketches for documented paintings – there are barely eight signed and dated paintings currently known – makes it difficult to follow the development of his works on paper. Tracing the evolution of Castiglione's style throughout his career is particularly hard, for several factors are concurrently at work: his inherent vacillation between his own personal urges and a more dispassionate adherence to nature, the range of his responses to other artists that he was looking at, and the changes in style that resulted from varying his technique. The best way to understand the chronology of Castiglione's drawings, then, is to imagine how individual sheets might reflect the evolution of his efforts to paint in oils with boar-bristle brushes directly onto paper. His challenge was to distinguish every individual figure, to make actions and emotional states defined and believable, without laboring his draftsmanship. His intention was to cultivate an elegant style of painting while drawing (or, conversely, of drawing while painting) without abandoning the emotional and formal content. Moreover, the chronology of Castiglione's oil drawings might be suggested by his degree of success at balancing dry and wet contours, at conveying a sense of volume and spatial differentiation between his figures, and at arranging his individual figures and motifs into multi-figure compositions.

Timothy J. Standring

Study of Trees, with Two Figures on the Right

ca. 1650 · pen and brown ink · 27.4 × 41.7 cm
National Galleries of Scotland. David Laing Bequest
to the Royal Scottish Academy on loan 1966

Pastoral Landscape

ca. 1645–1650 · pen and brown ink, and wash · 27.2 × 41 cm
Staatsgalerie Stuttgart, Graphische Sammlung, alter Bestand

The Finding of Cyrus

ca. 1655–1660 · brush drawing, red-brown oil paint with
green, red, blue-gray, grayish-pink, and white touches · 34.5 × 24 cm
The Royal Collection / HM Queen Elizabeth II

Noah Leading the Animals into the Ark

ca. 1655–1660 · brush drawing, red-brown oil paint with
blue-gray touches · 31.1 × 26.1 cm
The Royal Collection / HM Queen Elizabeth II

Diana Resting under a Tree by a Herm

ca. 1645–1650 · brush drawing, brown and red-brown oil paint
with red, green, blue, pink, and white touches · 27.5 × 40 cm
Albertina, Vienna

Orpheus Charming the Animals

ca. 1645 · brush drawing, brown and red-brown
oil paint with green and blue touches · 35 × 49 cm
Staatsgalerie Stuttgart, Graphische Sammlung,
loan 1976 Collection Schloss Fachsenfeld

7

Jacob's Return

ca. 1640–1645 · brush drawing, brown
and red-brown oil paint · 31 × 44 cm
Albertina, Vienna

**Shepherds and Shepherdesses with
a Flock at the Watering Place**

early 1630s · brush drawing, brown and red-brown oil paint
with mauve and blue touches, brown and red-brown chalk · 26.5 × 39 cm
Städel Museum, Frankfurt am Main

Woman with Child Riding on a Donkey,
a Young Man Walking Alongside

ca. 1635–1640 · brush drawing, brown and red-brown oil paint · 30.3 × 38.5 cm
Städel Museum, Frankfurt am Main

Noah Leading the Animals into the Ark

ca. 1660 · brush drawing, brown and red-brown oil paint with
gray and blue-gray touches · 32 × 45.4 cm
Kunsthaus Zürich, Collection of Prints and Drawings, 1945

Two Men in front of a Field Camp

ca. 1650–1660 · brush drawing, brown-orange oil paint with
green-gray touches · 27.6 × 40 cm
The Jan Krugier Foundation, Switzerland

The Israelites in the Wilderness (?)

ca. 1640–1645 · brush drawing, red-brown oil paint · 29.4 × 41.2 cm
The Royal Collection / HM Queen Elizabeth II

13

Rachel Hiding the Idols

ca. 1650–1655 · brush drawing, brown
and red-brown oil paint with
dark yellow, white, blue, red, green,
and gray touches · 27.1 × 40.6 cm
National Galleries of Scotland.
David Laing Bequest to the Royal Scottish
Academy transferred 1910

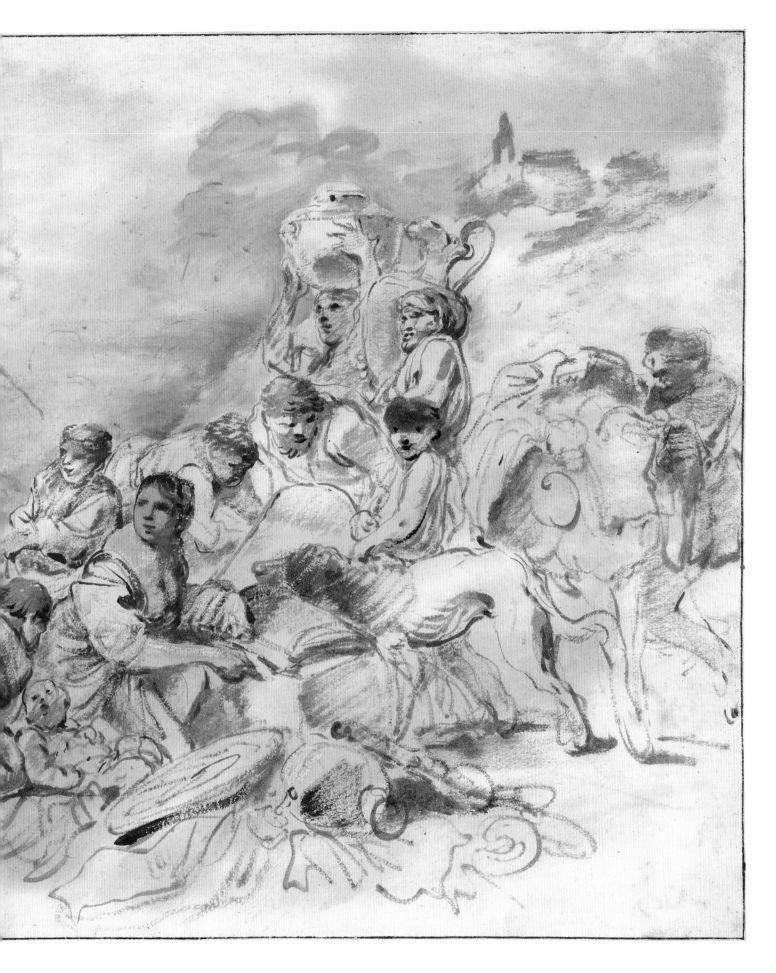

An Allegory of the Eucharist

ca. 1660 · brush drawing, red-brown oil paint with blue
and white touches, bister · 44 × 68.5 cm
Staatliche Graphische Sammlung München

Christ on the Cross, Saint John the Evangelist, and the Holy Women

ca. 1650–1655 · brush drawing, brown and black oil paint with red,
green, yellow, blue, and white touches, pen and brown ink · 42.3 × 29 cm
Musée des Beaux-Arts de Lyon

Hagar and Ismael in the Desert

1655–1660 · brush drawing, brown oil paint with blue-gray
and red touches · 43.6 × 31.9 cm
Kupferstichkabinett, Staatliche Museen zu Berlin

The Expulsion of Hagar

late 1640s · brush drawing, brown and red-brown oil paint
with green, blue-green, white, and bluish-white touches · 39 × 27.5 cm
The Devonshire Collections

God Appearing to Jacob in Bethel

ca. 1647–1650 · brush drawing,
brown oil paint with gray, red, blue,
and white touches · 28.4 × 41.6 cm
Kupferstichkabinett, Staatliche Museen
zu Berlin

Saint Jerome in Meditation

ca. 1655–1660 · brush drawing, red-brown oil paint with
grayish-blue touches · 33.9 × 27.1 cm
Hessisches Landesmuseum Darmstadt

Preaching of Saint John the Baptist

late 1650s · brush drawing, red-brown oil paint with
blue-gray touches · 40 × 28.5 cm
The Courtauld, London (Samuel Courtauld Trust)

The Rest on the Flight into Egypt

1650–1655 · brush drawing, brown and red-brown oil paint with
blue and white touches · 28.4 × 39.8 cm
Fondation Custodia, Collection Frits Lugt, Paris

The Rest on the Flight into Egypt

ca. 1648 · brush drawing, brown ink and oil paint with
blue and gray touches · 37.1 × 27.1 cm
Collection Museum Boijmans Van Beuningen, Rotterdam

The Adoration of the Shepherds

ca. 1640–1645 · brush drawing, brown and
red-brown oil paint · 42.2 × 56.7 cm
Albertina, Vienna

The Adoration of the Magi

ca. 1650–1655 · brush drawing, red-brown
oil paint · 41.7 × 57.3 cm
The Royal Collection / HM Queen Elizabeth II

The Choice of Hercules

ca. 1655–1660 · brush drawing, red-brown oil paint
with blue-gray touches · 33.8 × 25.8 cm
The Royal Collection / HM Queen Elizabeth II

A Scene from "The Golden Ass" of Apuleius

ca. 1660 · brush drawing, red-brown oil paint
with blue touches · 40 × 57.4 cm
Hamburger Kunsthalle, Kupferstichkabinett

Circe with the Companions of
Odysseus Transformed into Animals

ca. 1650–1655 · brush drawing, brown and
red-brown oil paint · 39.4 × 56 cm
The Royal Collection / HM Queen Elizabeth II

Circe

ca. 1650–1655 · pen and brown ink · 19.8 × 28 cm
Hessisches Landesmuseum Darmstadt

Circe

ca. 1645–1650 · pen and brown ink · 22.8 × 20.6 cm
Fondation Custodia, Collection Frits Lugt, Paris

Historical Scene: Three Figures Kneeling before a Sovereign and Soldiers

ca. 1640–1650 · pen and brown ink · 28.2 × 25.5 cm

Musée du Louvre, Département des Arts graphiques, Paris

A Black Page Holding Hounds in a Landscape

ca. 1650–1655 · brush drawing, red-brown
oil paint · 41.2 × 55.7 cm
The Royal Collection / HM Queen Elizabeth II

Omnia Vanitas

ca. 1650–1655 · brush drawing, dark reddish-brown
oil paint · 39.2 × 54.4 cm
The Royal Collection / HM Queen Elizabeth II

An Allegory in Honor of the Duchess of Mantua

ca. 1650–1655 · brush drawing, dark reddish-brown
and dark red oil paint · 39.2 × 54.9 cm
The Royal Collection / HM Queen Elizabeth II

**Study for an Allegory in Honor
of the Ruling Couple of Mantua**

1652–1655 · pen and brown ink, and wash · 25.7 × 38.3 cm
Hamburger Kunsthalle, Kupferstichkabinett

**An Allegory in Honor of
the Duchess of Mantua**

after 1652 · pen and brown ink, and wash · 25.5 × 19.5 cm
Victoria and Albert Museum, London

Study for an Allegory on Human Culture

ca. 1652 · brush drawing, red chalk, brown ink, blue,
white, and black oil paint · 47.5 × 36 cm
Hamburger Kunsthalle, Kupferstichkabinett

The Blind Leading the Blind

ca. 1650 · pen and brown ink, and
brownish-gray wash · 26.4×38.4 cm
The Courtauld, London (Samuel Courtauld Trust)

Nymph Surprised by Satyrs

ca. 1655 · brush drawing, red-brown and brown oil paint with blue, green,
bluish-green, mauve, and bluish-white touches, bister · 42 × 53 cm
Victoria and Albert Museum, London. Bequeathed by Rev. Alexander Dyce

Sacred and Profane Love

ca. 1635 · brush drawing, brown and red-brown
oil paint with red and blue-gray touches · 21.6 × 29.5 cm
The Royal Collection / HM Queen Elizabeth II

Women and Children Praying before a Tomb

ca. 1640–1645 · brush drawing, red-brown oil paint · 55.2 × 40 cm
The Royal Collection / HM Queen Elizabeth II

The Saving of the Infant Pyrrhus

ca. 1635–1640 · brush drawing, brown oil paint · 26 × 37.8 cm
The Royal Collection / HM Queen Elizabeth II

David before Saul

after 1648 · brush drawing, brown
and red-brown oil paint · 22.1 × 33.4 cm
Beaux-Arts de Paris

103

43

A Potentate, Carrying a Mace and a Sword, Half Length

ca. 1655–1660 · brush drawing, brown and red-brown
oil paint with blue touches · 24 × 17.4 cm
Fondation Custodia, Collection Frits Lugt, Paris

The Head of a Youth in a Turban

ca. 1645–1650 · red chalk · 16.5 × 14 cm
The Royal Collection / HM Queen Elizabeth II

Monotypes

Castiglione was – unusually for his time – a crossover artist working in a variety of media. His sketches executed with brush and oil blur the line separating drawing from painting, and the monotype technique which he inaugurated was an equally indeterminate medium of expression, producing images that cannot be categorized unambiguously as either drawings or prints. To create a monotype, the design is laid down on an inked printing plate, while the plate itself remains unaltered. As a consequence, the monotype technique produces only a single genuinely saturated impression, usually by passing plate and paper through a press. Although the paper does receive the greater part of the ink during the printing process, enough ink may remain on the plate to produce a second impression, which will, however, be paler, hence the term "ghost" impression (see cat. 50). Left unscored, the printing plate is thus reusable, and can produce a large number of different monotypes.

Given the simplicity of the process, it seems likely that works with monotype characteristics were produced long before Castiglione's lifetime. A precondition for the development of the monotype into an autonomous expressive resource, however, was the emergence of a new understanding of printmaking techniques as a field for creative experimentation that transcended mere reproductive purposes.

Surviving from Castiglione's hand are circa two dozen monotypes. Their examination leads to a distinction between two different approaches to the application of ink to the printing plate: in the first, the motif was sketched directly onto the plate (the so-called "light-field" technique). To date, altogether nine monotypes produced with this technique have been documented (among them *The Head of an Oriental* from the Royal Collection that is included in the present exhibition; cat. 45). Most of these compositions were executed using broad brushstrokes. Where the ink was applied too thickly, the printing process may result in a puckered effect; it is not always clear whether these were intended by the artist.

The second approach is the "dark-field" technique, which clearly predominates among Castiglione's monotypes. Here, a brush or roller was used to spread the ink evenly across the metal plate, resulting in a uniformly dark surface. Castiglione then scratched lines into the dark film of viscous ink so that they showed up as impactful bright streaks and lighter passages against the dark ground. To scratch out ink from the desired areas, Castiglione used wooden sticks of various widths, which he applied with varying degrees of pressure. Unlike metal needles, these implements did not permanently mark the plate when the composition was being laid down. At the same time, larger areas were brightened through the use of wiping techniques; here, the printing ink was removed using the tip of a rag, soft brushes, or even the artist's fingers. The use of wiping to remove printing ink allowed Castiglione to generate half-tones.

Incidentally, the monotypes produced using the "dark-field" technique often betray commonalities with works by Rembrandt, whom Castiglione admired greatly. Although Rembrandt seems to have produced no monotypes, he did employ comparable effects by deliberately covering the plate with gradations of ink, known as plate tone (cat. 51).

There can be little doubt that the magic of the monotype resides in its rapid execution on the plate, in its powerful effects of light and dark, and in outcomes that often harbor surprises for the artist himself. As the artist Charles Alvah Walker once observed about this printing technique, used so extensively during the nineteenth and twentieth centuries: "Straightforwardness is the foundation of the monotype."

Jonas Beyer

The Head of an Oriental

ca. 1645–1650 · monotype with black oil paint,
and brown wash · 31.7 × 23.6 cm
The Royal Collection / HM Queen Elizabeth II

Rembrandt van Rijn (1606–1669)

Bearded Old Man in a High Fur Cap, with Eyes Closed

ca. 1635 · etching · plate: 11.3 × 10.4 cm
Musée Jenisch Vevey – Cabinet cantonal des estampes, Fondation William
Cuendet & Atelier de Saint-Prex, don inaliénable de la famille Cuendet

Rembrandt van Rijn (1606–1669)

The Angel Appearing to the Shepherds

1634 · etching, drypoint, and engraving · plate: 26.2 × 21.8 cm
Graphische Sammlung ETH Zürich

The Annunciation to the Shepherds

1650−1655 · monotype · 37.2×24.6 cm
Albertina, Vienna

The Nativity with Angels and God the Father

ca. 1655 · monotype, first pull · 36.8 × 25.4 cm
Bibliothèque nationale de France, Paris

50

The Nativity with Angels and God the Father

ca. 1655 · monotype, second pull · 36.8 × 25.4 cm
The Royal Collection / HM Queen Elizabeth II

51
Rembrandt van Rijn (1606–1669)

The Entombment

ca. 1654 · etching and drypoint, plate tone · plate: 21.1×16.1 cm
Graphische Sammlung ETH Zürich

The Raising of Lazarus

ca. 1647 – mid-1650s · monotype · 19.7 × 27.9 cm
Albertina, Vienna

A Herd Fording a Stream

late 1640s · monotype · 20.8×31.7 cm
Bibliothèque nationale de France, Paris

Christ on the Cross

ca. 1650–1655 · monotype · 38.7 × 26.6 cm
Bibliothèque nationale de France, Paris

Etchings

Quite a few painters tried their hand at etching after the technique was first practiced in the early sixteenth century. Although it was generally associated with northern European art, there were also many Italians who produced etchings such as Il Parmigianino, Federico Barocci, and Annibale Carracci, among others, but their interest was normally short-lived. This was not, however, the case with Giovanni Benedetto Castiglione, who produced a serious and much-appreciated print oeuvre.

To make an etching, a copperplate is first covered with a ground consisting of some sort of wax, into which the artist scratches with a needle to expose the metal beneath where a line is desired. The plate is then dipped into an acid bath, thus exposing these unprotected parts to the corrosive acid, which bites out lines in the copper. The plate is then taken out of the acid and the wax layer removed: the copperplate is now ready for printing. This is done by inking the plate and wiping it so that ink only remains in the etched furrows. A sheet of damp paper is then put on the inked plate and the two are pulled through a rolling press together, causing the paper to suck out the ink from the lines. The result is a mirror image of the subject etched in the copperplate.

When exactly Castiglione began producing his etchings is unclear and the issue of dating them is still problematic. While most of his etchings are not dated, some professional publishers of his copperplates in Rome, namely Giovanni Domenico de Rossi and Gian Giacomo de Rossi, inscribed dates onto the plates themselves. Moreover, attempts to date Castiglione's prints in relation to his paintings and drawings have been equally vexing, since he often revisited subjects and we do not know if his prints were produced prior to or after his drawings and paintings. For example, a drawing closely linked to a painting could have been used for an etching much later in his career. In any case, given the considerable logistics needed to produce an etching, it seems that Castiglione produced the main body of his etchings over a few short periods of activity, with, as far as one can see, rather subtle changes in his stylistic and technical development.

The creative part of making an etching is akin to drawing: to draw with an etching needle on the wax surface is much like flourishing a reed pen across a sheet of paper. However, this indirect way of creating a work of art is not so easy after all, as some of Castiglione's prints reveal. Much could go wrong. Whenever he failed to scratch his needle deep enough into the wax, his drawn line failed to bite sufficiently, leaving an inadvertently masked-out blank patch, for example, on Diogenes left arm in *Diogenes Searching for an Honest Man* (cat. 65). If part of the layer of wax came off during the etching process, it would cause an area of indiscriminate "foul biting," which is evidently what happened in the lower center in *The Adoration of the Infant Christ* (p. 19). And when a plate was not properly polished before use, there was a risk of scratches and other imperfections showing through in the final result.

Moreover, the practical logistics required of making an etching involved considerable investment in both time and money: buying a copperplate; polishing it; mixing the right ingredients for the etching ground, the acid, and the ink; hiring a professional printer; and setting up a network for the distribution of the prints. Subsequently, many *peintres-graveurs* were discouraged after just a few attempts in the medium because the investments, either in time or money, did not pay off. To our good fortune, however, Castiglione persisted.

His use of the etching technique is quite basic, with mostly only a single etching bath for the copperplate. Through his ingenious distribution of lighter and darker passages, he was able to create more lively and exciting compositions than, for instance, his contemporary Pietro Testa. This ingenious elementary handling of light and dark can be recognized in etchings such as *Tobit Burying the Dead* (cat. 69). Castiglione used mainly etched hatchings in combination with the white of the paper. He also used networks of cross-hatching that did not follow the contours of the individual elements in the composition but instead covered whole passages in order to darken them, for instance in the upper left of *The Finding of the Bodies of Saints Peter and Paul* (cat. 70). By using the etching technique in such an exemplary way, Castiglione made a considerable number of very exciting etchings that certainly stand out in the history of Italian printmaking.

Jaco Rutgers

A Presumed Self-Portrait

late 1640s · etching · plate: 18.8 × 13.8 cm
Musée Jenisch Vevey – Cabinet cantonal des estampes,
collection de l'Etat de Vaud

56

Rembrandt van Rijn (1606–1669)

Self-Portrait in a Cap and Scarf with the Face Dark

1633 · etching · plate: 13.2 × 10.3 cm
MAH Musée d'art et d'histoire, Ville de Genève. Ancien fonds

57

Jan Lievens (1607–1674)

Bust of an Oriental with Feathered Turban

ca. 1630 · etching and drypoint · plate: 27.4 × 22.5 cm
Graphische Sammlung ETH Zürich

58

Man with a Mustache, Wearing a Fur Headdress, Facing Left, from Large Oriental Heads

late 1640s · etching · plate: 18 × 14.5 cm
Musée Jenisch Vevey – Cabinet cantonal des estampes,
collection de l'Etat de Vaud

**Man with a Long Beard, Wearing a Headdress and
Fur Cap, Facing Right**, from **Large Oriental Heads**

late 1640s · etching · plate: 18.5 × 13.4 cm
Musée Jenisch Vevey – Cabinet cantonal des estampes,
collection de l'Etat de Vaud

Man with a Beard and Mustache, Wearing a Tasseled Headdress, Facing Left, from **Large Oriental Heads**

late 1640s · etching · plate: 18 × 15 cm
Musée Jenisch Vevey – Cabinet cantonal des estampes,
collection de l'Etat de Vaud

**Bearded Old Man with His Head Leaning
Forward**, from **Large Oriental Heads**

late 1640s · etching · plate: 18 × 15 cm
Musée Jenisch Vevey – Cabinet cantonal des
estampes, collection de l'Etat de Vaud

Man Wearing a Plumed Fur Cap and a Scarf,
from **Large Oriental Heads**

late 1640s · etching · plate: 18 × 14.5 cm
Musée Jenisch Vevey – Cabinet cantonal des estampes,
collection de l'Etat de Vaud

Man Holding a Large Banderole,
from **Small Oriental Heads**

late 1640s · etching · plate: 10.8 × 8.1 cm
Private collection

64

Rembrandt van Rijn (1606–1669)

Old Man Shading His Eyes with His Hand

ca. 1639 · etching and drypoint · plate: 13.8 × 11.3 cm
MAH Musée d'art et d'histoire, Ville de Genève. Ancien fonds

Diogenes Searching for an Honest Man

ca. 1645–1647 · etching · plate: 21.8×30.4 cm

MAH Musée d'art et d'histoire, Ville de Genève. Ancien fonds

Al Sig: Nicolo Simonelli Mio Sig

on tanta glo ria serba piu uirtuo che mai le sue memorie baldanzoso risorge al mondo co delineamenti
he so quanto ella lumi ti ne suoi uirtuosi Costumi o particolarm ente nel cercar con la lanterna gli huomini ho giudicato che il dedicarlo a lei sara un
altro non discorderanno saluo che esso pote con tanta Seuerita disprezzarei fauori d'un Alessandro e V.S. per superarlo ne gli atti della benignita sapra con
ssequi della mia deuotione la quale riuara la riuerisco

Amico e Seruitore

G. D. R. D. D. C. D.

Si stampano in Roma per Gio Domenico Rossi alla Pace al Insegne a Parigi

Temporalis Aeternitas

1645 · etching · plate: 30.3×20.6 cm
MAH Musée d'art et d'histoire, Ville de Genève.
Ancien fonds

The Genius of Castiglione

before 1648 · etching · plate: 37 × 24.9 cm
Musée Jenisch Vevey – Cabinet cantonal des
estampes, collection de l'Etat de Vaud

Circe with the Companions of Odysseus Transformed into Animals

1650–1651 · etching · plate: 21.8 × 31.1 cm

Graphische Sammlung ETH Zürich

Tobit Burying the Dead

ca. 1647 – mid-1650s · etching · plate: 20.3 × 29.4 cm
Musée Jenisch Vevey – Cabinet cantonal des estampes,
collection de l'Etat de Vaud

70

The Finding of the Bodies of Saints Peter and Paul

ca. 1647 – mid-1650s · etching · plate: 30.2 × 20.7 cm
Kunsthaus Zürich, Collection of Prints and Drawings, 2020

The Raising of Lazarus

ca. 1647–mid-1650s · etching · plate: 22.4 × 31.6 cm
Graphische Sammlung ETH Zürich

CASTILIONE GENOVESE P

The Nativity with God the Father and Angels

after 1647 · etching · plate: 20 × 39.5 cm
Musée Jenisch Vevey – Cabinet cantonal des estampes,
collection de l'Etat de Vaud

The Entry of the Animals into the Ark

1650–1655 · etching · plate: 20.7 × 40.2 cm
Graphische Sammlung ETH Zürich

**A Pagan Sacrifice in the
Temple of Jerusalem**

ca. 1645–1650 · oil on canvas · 43.2 × 77.4 cm
Private collection

Appendix

List of Exhibited Works

Listed in order of their appearance; unless stated otherwise, by Giovanni Benedetto Castiglione, called Il Grechetto (1609–1664).

Cat. 1, p. 58
Study of Trees, with Two Figures on the Right
ca. 1650
Pen and brown ink, 27.4 × 41.7 cm
National Galleries of Scotland.
David Laing Bequest to the Royal Scottish Academy on loan 1966
RSA 198

Cat. 2, p. 59
Pastoral Landscape
ca. 1645–1650
Pen and brown ink, and wash, 27.2 × 41 cm
Staatsgalerie Stuttgart,
Graphische Sammlung, alter Bestand
C1922/68

Cat. 3, p. 60
The Finding of Cyrus
ca. 1655–1660
Brush drawing, red-brown oil paint with green, red, blue-gray, grayish-pink, and white touches, 34.5 × 24 cm
The Royal Collection / HM Queen Elizabeth II
RCIN 903953

Cat. 4, p. 61
Noah Leading the Animals into the Ark
ca. 1655–1660
Brush drawing, red-brown oil paint with blue-gray touches, 31.1 × 26.1 cm
The Royal Collection / HM Queen Elizabeth II
RCIN 903951

Cat. 5, p. 62
Diana Resting under a Tree by a Herm
ca. 1645–1650
Brush drawing, brown and red-brown oil paint with red, green, blue, pink, and white touches, 27.5 × 40 cm
Albertina, Vienna
2852

Cat. 6, p. 63
Orpheus Charming the Animals
ca. 1645
Brush drawing, brown and red-brown oil paint with green and blue touches, 35 × 49 cm
Staatsgalerie Stuttgart, Graphische Sammlung, loan 1976 Collection Schloss Fachsenfeld
SF III/532

Cat. 7, p. 64
Jacob's Return
ca. 1640–1645
Brush drawing, brown and red-brown oil paint, 31 × 44 cm
Albertina, Vienna
2844

Cat. 8, p. 65
Shepherds and Shepherdesses with a Flock at the Watering Place
early 1630s
Brush drawing, brown and red-brown oil paint with mauve and blue touches, brown and red-brown chalk, 26.5 × 39 cm
Städel Museum, Frankfurt am Main
4095

Cat. 9, p. 66
Woman with Child Riding on a Donkey, a Young Man Walking Alongside
ca. 1635–1640
Brush drawing, brown and red-brown oil paint, 30.3 × 38.5 cm
Städel Museum, Frankfurt am Main
4090

Cat. 10, p. 67
Noah Leading the Animals into the Ark
ca. 1660
Brush drawing, brown and red-brown oil paint with gray and blue-gray touches, 32 × 45.4 cm
Kunsthaus Zürich, Collection of Prints and Drawings, 1945
Z.1945/0007

Cat. 11, p. 68
Two Men in front of a Field Camp
ca. 1650–1660
Brush drawing, brown-orange oil paint with green-gray touches, 27.6 × 40 cm
The Jan Krugier Foundation, Switzerland
FJK 027

Cat. 12, p. 69
The Israelites in the Wilderness (?)
ca. 1640–1645
Brush drawing, red-brown oil paint, 29.4 × 41.2 cm
The Royal Collection / HM Queen Elizabeth II
RCIN 903856

Cat. 13, pp. 70–71
Rachel Hiding the Idols
ca. 1650–1655
Brush drawing, brown and red-brown oil paint with dark yellow, white, blue, red, green, and gray touches, 27.1 × 40.6 cm
National Galleries of Scotland.
David Laing Bequest to the Royal Scottish Academy transferred 1910
D 700

Cat. 14, p. 72
An Allegory of the Eucharist
ca. 1660
Brush drawing, red-brown oil paint with blue and white touches, bister, 44 × 68.5 cm
Staatliche Graphische Sammlung München
1909:1 Z

Cat. 15, p. 73
Christ on the Cross, Saint John the Evangelist, and the Holy Women
ca. 1650–1655
Brush drawing, brown and black oil paint with red, green, yellow, blue, and white touches, pen and brown ink, 42.3 × 29 cm
Musée des Beaux-Arts de Lyon
B 392

Cat. 38, p. 97
Nymph Surprised by Satyrs
ca. 1655
Brush drawing, red-brown and brown oil paint
with blue, green, bluish-green, mauve, and
bluish-white touches, bister, 42 × 53 cm
Victoria and Albert Museum, London.
Bequeathed by Rev. Alexander Dyce
DYCE.347

Cat. 39, pp. 98–99
Sacred and Profane Love
ca. 1635
Brush drawing, brown and red-brown oil paint
with red and blue-gray touches, 21.6 × 29.5 cm
The Royal Collection / HM Queen Elizabeth II
RCIN 903899

Cat. 40, p. 100
**Women and Children Praying before
a Tomb**
ca. 1640–1645
Brush drawing, red-brown oil paint,
55.2 × 40 cm
The Royal Collection / HM Queen Elizabeth II
RCIN 904081

Cat. 41, p. 101
The Saving of the Infant Pyrrhus
ca. 1635–1640
Brush drawing, brown oil paint, 26 × 37.8 cm
The Royal Collection / HM Queen Elizabeth II
RCIN 904018

Cat. 42, pp. 102–103
David before Saul
after 1648
Brush drawing, brown and red-brown oil paint,
22.1 × 33.4 cm
Beaux-Arts de Paris
2296

Cat. 43, p. 104
**A Potentate, Carrying a Mace and a Sword,
Half Length**
ca. 1655–1660
Brush drawing, brown and red-brown oil paint
with blue touches, 24 × 17.4 cm
Fondation Custodia, Collection Frits Lugt, Paris
4397

Cat. 44, p. 105
The Head of a Youth in a Turban
ca. 1645–1650
Red chalk, 16.5 × 14 cm
The Royal Collection / HM Queen Elizabeth II
RCIN 903947

Cat. 45, p. 108
The Head of an Oriental
ca. 1645–1650
Monotype with black oil paint, and brown wash,
31.7 × 23.6 cm
The Royal Collection / HM Queen Elizabeth II
RCIN 903946

Cat. 46, p. 109
Rembrandt van Rijn (1606–1669)
**Bearded Old Man in a High Fur Cap,
with Eyes Closed**
ca. 1635
Etching, plate: 11.3 × 10.4 cm
Musée Jenisch Vevey – Cabinet cantonal des
estampes, Fondation William Cuendet & Atelier
de Saint-Prex, don inaliénable de la famille
Cuendet
FWC&ASP-1978-0165

Cat. 47, p. 110
Rembrandt van Rijn (1606–1669)
The Angel Appearing to the Shepherds
1634
Etching, drypoint and, engraving,
plate: 26.2 × 21.8 cm
Graphische Sammlung ETH Zürich
D 814

Cat. 48, p. 111
The Annunciation to the Shepherds
1650–1655
Monotype, 37.2 × 24.6 cm
Albertina, Vienna
DG2003/337

Cat. 49, p. 112
**The Nativity with Angels and God
the Father**
ca. 1655
Monotype, first pull, 36.8 × 25.4 cm
Bibliothèque nationale de France, Paris
ESTNUM 2021-56

Cat. 50, p. 113
**The Nativity with Angels and God
the Father**
ca. 1655
Monotype, second pull, 36.8 × 25.4 cm
The Royal Collection / HM Queen Elizabeth II
RCIN 970068

Cat. 51, p. 114
Rembrandt van Rijn (1606–1669)
The Entombment
ca. 1654
Etching and drypoint, plate tone,
plate: 21.1 × 16.1 cm
Graphische Sammlung ETH Zürich
D 5078

Cat. 52, p. 115
The Raising of Lazarus
ca. 1647–mid-1650s
Monotype, 19.7 × 27.9 cm
Albertina, Vienna
DG2003/340

Cat. 53, p. 116
A Herd Fording a Stream
late 1640s
Monotype, 20.8 × 31.7 cm
Bibliothèque nationale de France, Paris
ESTNUM 2021-58

Cat. 54, p. 117
Christ on the Cross
ca. 1650–1655
Monotype, 38.7 × 26.6 cm
Bibliothèque nationale de France, Paris
ESTNUM 2021-57

Cat. 55, p. 120
A Presumed Self-Portrait
late 1640s
Etching, plate: 18.5 × 13.3 cm
Musée Jenisch Vevey – Cabinet cantonal des
estampes, collection de l'Etat de Vaud
VD 000-0013.6

Cat. 56, p. 121
Rembrandt van Rijn (1606–1669)
**Self-Portrait in a Cap and Scarf with
the Face Dark**
1633
Etching, plate: 13.2 × 10.3 cm
MAH Musée d'art et d'histoire, Ville de Genève.
Ancien fonds
E 2004-0110

Cat. 57, p. 122
Jan Lievens (1607–1674)
Bust of an Oriental with Feathered Turban
ca. 1630
Etching and drypoint, plate: 27.4 × 22.5 cm
Graphische Sammlung ETH Zürich
D 5629

Cat. 58, p. 123
**Man with a Mustache, Wearing
a Fur Headdress, Facing Left,** from
Large Oriental Heads
late 1640s
Etching, plate: 18 × 14.5 cm
Musée Jenisch Vevey – Cabinet cantonal des
estampes, collection de l'Etat de Vaud
VD 000-0013.4

Cat. 59, p. 124
**Man with a Long Beard, Wearing a
Headdress and Fur Cap, Facing Right**, from
Large Oriental Heads
late 1640s
Etching, plate: 18.5 × 13.4 cm
Musée Jenisch Vevey – Cabinet cantonal des
estampes, collection de l'Etat de Vaud
VD 000-0013.2

Cat. 60, p. 125
**Man with a Beard and Mustache,
Wearing a Tasseled Headdress,
Facing Left**, from **Large Oriental Heads**
late 1640s
Etching, plate: 18 × 15 cm
Musée Jenisch Vevey – Cabinet cantonal des
estampes, collection de l'Etat de Vaud
VD 000-0013.1

Cat. 61, p. 126
**Bearded Old Man with His Head Leaning
Forward**, from **Large Oriental Heads**
late 1640s
Etching, plate: 18 × 15 cm
Musée Jenisch Vevey – Cabinet cantonal des
estampes, collection de l'Etat de Vaud
VD 000-0013.5

Cat. 62, p. 127
Man Wearing a Plumed Fur Cap and a Scarf,
from **Large Oriental Heads**
late 1640s
Etching, plate: 18 × 14.5 cm
Musée Jenisch Vevey – Cabinet cantonal des
estampes, collection de l'Etat de Vaud
VD 000-0013.3

Cat. 63, p. 128
Man Holding a Large Banderole, from
Small Oriental Heads
late 1640s
Etching, plate: 10.8 × 8.1 cm
Private collection

Cat. 64, p. 129
Rembrandt van Rijn (1606–1669)
Old Man Shading His Eyes with His Hand
ca. 1639
Etching and drypoint, plate: 13.8 × 11.3 cm
MAH Musée d'art et d'histoire, Ville de Genève.
Ancien fonds
E 2009-0002

Cat. 65, pp. 130–131
Diogenes Searching for an Honest Man
ca. 1645–1647
Etching, plate: 21.8 × 30.4 cm
MAH Musée d'art et d'histoire, Ville de Genève.
Ancien fonds
E 2011-1793

Cat. 66, p. 132
Temporalis Aeternitas
1645
Etching, plate: 30.3 × 20.6 cm
MAH Musée d'art et d'histoire, Ville de Genève.
Ancien fonds
E 2011-2292

Cat. 67, p. 133
The Genius of Castiglione
before 1648
Etching, plate: 37 × 24.9 cm
Musée Jenisch Vevey – Cabinet cantonal des
estampes, collection de l'Etat de Vaud
VD 998-0002

Cat. 68, pp. 134–135
**Circe with the Companions of Odysseus
Transformed into Animals**
1650–1651
Etching, plate: 21.8 × 31.1 cm
Graphische Sammlung ETH Zürich
D 10137

Cat. 69, p. 136
Tobit Burying the Dead
ca. 1647–mid-1650s
Etching, plate: 20.3 × 29.4 cm
Musée Jenisch Vevey – Cabinet cantonal des
estampes, collection de l'Etat de Vaud
VD 997-0010

Cat. 70, p. 137
**The Finding of the Bodies of Saints Peter
and Paul**
ca. 1647–mid-1650s
Etching, plate: 30.2 × 20.7 cm
Kunsthaus Zürich, Collection of Prints and
Drawings, 2020
ZKG.2020/0001

Cat. 71, pp. 138–139
The Raising of Lazarus
ca. 1647–mid-1650s
Etching, plate: 22.4 × 31.6 cm
Graphische Sammlung ETH Zürich
D 28739

Cat. 72, p. 140
The Nativity with God the Father and Angels
after 1647
Etching, plate: 20 × 39.5 cm
Musée Jenisch Vevey – Cabinet cantonal des
estampes, collection de l'Etat de Vaud
VD 018-0015

Cat. 73, p. 141
The Entry of the Animals into the Ark
1650–1655
Etching, plate: 20.7 × 40.2 cm
Graphische Sammlung ETH Zürich
D 1029

Cat. 74, p. 143
**A Pagan Sacrifice in the Temple
of Jerusalem**
ca. 1645–1650
Oil on canvas, 43.2 × 77.4 cm
Private collection

Cat. 75 (not illustrated in the catalog)
A Presumed Self-Portrait
late 1640s
Etching, plate: 18.8 × 13.8 cm
Collection Peter F. Carls

Cat. 76 (not illustrated in the catalog)
Rembrandt van Rijn (1606–1669)
The Entombment
ca. 1654
Etching, engraving, and drypoint,
plate: 21.1 × 16.1 cm
Musée Jenisch Vevey – Cabinet cantonal des
estampes, Fondation William Cuendet & Atelier
de Saint-Prex, don inaliénable de la famille
Cuendet
FWC&ASP-1978-0146

Selected Bibliography

Abbreviations

TIB = *The Illustrated Bartsch: Italian Masters of the Seventeenth Century*, ed. Paolo Bellini, vol. 46 (Commentary), New York 1985.

NH = *The New Hollstein Dutch and Flemish Etchings, Engravings and Woodcuts 1450–1700: Rembrandt*, vols. 1–2 (text) and 3–5 (plates), ed. Erik Hinterding and Jaco Rutgers, Ouderkerk aan den IJssel 2013.

A

Albl 2014
Stefan Albl, "Nicolò Simonelli e i suoi rapporti con Castiglione, Mola, Rosa, Testa e altri," in Albl/Sganzerla/Weston 2014, pp. 81–96.

Albl/Canevari 2014
Stefan Albl and Angiola Canevari, "Pietro Testa e Socrate," in Albl/Sganzerla/Weston 2014, pp. 185–201.

Albl/Sganzerla/Weston 2014
Stefan Albl, Anita V. Sganzerla, and Giulia M. Weston (ed.), *I Pittori del Dissenso. Giovanni Benedetto Castiglione, Andrea de Leone, Pier Francesco Mola, Pietro Testa, Salvator Rosa*, Rome 2014.

Alfonso 1972
Luigi Alfonso, "Liguri Illustri: Gio. Benedetto Castiglione detto il Grechetto," in *La Berio*, vol. 12 (II), Genoa 1972, pp. 40–45.

B

Baldinucci 1681–1728
Filippo Baldinucci, *Notizie de' professori del disegno da Cimabue in qua*, 6 vols., Florence 1681–1728.

Bartsch 1821
Adam Bartsch, *Le Peintre-Graveur*, vol. 21 (Peintres ou dessinateurs italiens: Maîtres du dix-septième siècle), Vienna 1821 (1876).

Bätschmann 1997
Oskar Bätschmann, *Ausstellungskünstler: Kult und Karriere im modernen Kunstsystem*, Cologne 1997 (English trans. by Eileen Martin, as: *The Artist in the Modern World. A Conflict Between Market and Self-Expression*, Cologne 1997)

Baudi di Vesme 1963
Alessandro Baudi di Vesme, "Salvatore Castiglione," in *L'Arte in Piemonte dal XVI al XVIII Secolo*, vol. 1, Turin 1963, pp. 297–298.

Bellini 1982
Paolo Bellini, *L'opera incisa di Giovanni Benedetto Castiglione*, Milan 1982.

Belloni 1988
Venanzio Belloni, "1658–La Quadreria di Gio. Batt. Raggi," in *Scritti e Cose d'Arte Genovese*, Genoa 1988.

Bernheimer 1951
Richard Bernheimer, "Some Drawings by Benedetto Castiglione," in *Art Bulletin*, vol. 33, 1951, pp. 47–51.

Bertolotti 1884
Antonio Bertolotti, *Artisti subalpini in Roma nei secoli XV, XVI e XVII*, Mantua 1884 (1965).

Beyer 2010
Jonas Beyer, "Drucke von leichter Hand," in *Druckgraphik zwischen Reproduktion und Invention*, ed. Jasper Kettner, Christien Melzer, and Claudia Schnitzer, Berlin 2010, pp. 189–203.

de Bie 1661
Cornelis de Bie, *Het Gulden Cabinet van de Edel Vry Schilder-Const*, Antwerp 1661.

Binion 1983
Alice Binion, "Algarotti's Sagredo Inventory," in *Master Drawings*, vol. 21, 4 (winter 1983), pp. 392–396.

Birke/Kertész 1995
Veronika Birke and Janine Kertész, *Die Italienischen Zeichnungen der Albertina*, vol. 3, Vienna 1995.

Blanc 1858
Charles Blanc, *Le Trésor de la Curiosité*, Paris 1858.

Blanc 2017
Alexandra Blanc, "'Sculptor Ludens', l'estampe comme médium pictural. Production, enjeux et réception des eaux-fortes de Giovanni Benedetto Castiglione (1609–1664)," PhD diss., Université de Neuchâtel, 2017.

Blunt 1939–1940
Anthony Blunt, "A Poussin-Castiglione Problem: Classicism and the Picturesque in 17th Century Rome," in *Journal of the Warburg and Courtauld Institutes*, vol. 3, 1939–1940, pp. 142–147.

Blunt 1945
Anthony Blunt, "The Drawings of Giovanni Benedetto Castiglione," in *Journal of the Warburg and Courtauld Institutes*, vol. 8, 1945, pp. 161–174.

Blunt 1954
Anthony Blunt, *The Drawings of G. B. Castiglione & Stefano della Bella in the Collection of Her Majesty The Queen at Windsor Castle*, London 1954.

Blunt 1966
Anthony Blunt, *The Paintings of Nicolas Poussin: A Critical Catalogue*, London 1966.

Busch 1986
Werner Busch, "Goya und die Tradition des 'capriccio,'" in *Wie eindeutig ist ein Kunstwerk?* ed. Max Imdahl, Cologne 1986, pp. 41–73.

C

Calabi 1923
Augusto Calabi, "The Monotypes of G. B. Castiglione: Catalogue," in *The Print Collector's Quarterly*, vol. 10, 1923, pp. 223–253.

Calabi 1925
Augusto Calabi, "Castiglione's Monotypes: A Supplement," in *The Print Collector's Quarterly*, vol. 12, 1925, pp. 435–441.

Calabi 1930
Augusto Calabi, "Castiglione's Monotypes: A Second Supplement," in *The Print Collector's Quarterly*, vol. 17, 1930, pp. 299–301.

Castiglione 1656
Salvatore Castiglione, *Copia di lettera scritta dal Signor Salvator Castiglione nobile Genovese all'Illustrissimo, & Eccellentissimo Signor Gio. Filippo Spinola prencipe di Molfetta, &c. circa l'entrata, & accoglienze fatte dall'AA.RR. di Savoia alla Regina di Svecia nell'augusta città di Torino*, 19 fols., Turin 1656.

Cavazzini 2008
Patrizia Cavazzini, *Painting as Business in Early Seventeenth-Century Rome*, University Park, P. A. 2008.

Chaumelin 1865
Marius Chaumelin, "Giovanni-Benedetto Castiglione," in *Histoire des peintres de toutes les écoles*, ed. Charles Blanc, vol. 5, Paris 1865.

Cheng 2008
Sandra Cheng, "Il Bello dal Deforme: Caricature and Comic Drawings in Seventeenth-Century Italy," PhD diss., University of Delaware, 2008.

Ciliberto 2004
Piera Ciliberto, "Tradizione ed Interpretazione Letteraria, Magia ed Etica nelle Raffigurazioni di Circe di Giovanni Benedetto Castiglione il Grechetto," in *Rivista dell'Istituto Nazionale di Archeologia e Storia dell'Arte*, vol. 59, 2004, pp. 207–214.

Consagra 1988
Francesca Consagra, "The Marketing of Pietro Testa's 'Poetic Inventions,'" in *Pietro Testa, 1612–1650: Prints and Drawings* (exh. cat. Philadelphia/Cambridge, M.A.), ed. Elizabeth Cropper and Charles Dempsey, Philadelphia 1988, pp. 87–104.

Consagra 1993
Francesca Consagra, "The De Rossi Family Print Publishing Shop: A Study in the History of the Print Industry in Seventeenth-Century Rome," PhD diss., Johns Hopkins University, 1993.

D

Davis 1958
Hugh H. Davis, "Epitaphs and the Memory," in *The Classical Journal*, vol. 53, 4 (1958), pp. 169–176.

Della Porta 1627
Giambattista Della Porta, *Della Fisonomia dell'Huomo*, Padua 1627.

Delogu 1928
Giuseppe Delogu, *G. B. Castiglione detto il Grechetto*, Bologna 1928.

Desenfans 1802
Noel Joesph Desenfans, *A Descriptive Catalogue of some pictures of the different schools, purchased for His Majesty, the Late King of Poland*, London 1802.

Dezallier d'Argenville 1745–1752
Antoine Joseph Dezallier d'Argenville, *Abrégé de la vie des plus fameux peintres*, 4 vols., Paris 1745–1752.

Dillon 1976
Gianvittorio Dillon, "Un monotipo inedito di G.B. Castiglione," in *Il conoscitore di stampe*, vol. 31, March–April 1976, pp. 4–8.

Di Penta 2014
Miriam Di Penta, "Novità sul Soggiorno di Andrea De Leone a Roma (1630). Riflessioni sul rapporto con Nicolas Poussin, Pietro Testa, Andrea Sacchi e l'ambiente di Casa dal Pozzo," in Albl/Sganzerla/Weston 2014, pp. 59–79.

E

Eidelberg/Rowlands 1994
Martin Eidelberg and Eliot Wooldridge Rowlands, "The Dispersal of the Last Duke of Mantua's Paintings," in *Gazette des Beaux-Arts*, vol. 123, 136 (1994), pp. 207–294.

F

Félibien 1725
André Félibien, *Entretiens sur les vies et les ouvrages des plus excellens peintres, anciens et modernes*, 6 vols., Trevoux 1725 (1666–1688).

Ferrari 1986
Oreste Ferrari, "L'Iconografia dei filosofi antichi nella pittura del sec. XVII in Italia," in *Storia dell'Arte*, vol. 57, 1986, pp. 103–181.

Findlen 2004
Paula Findlen (ed.), *Athanasius Kircher: The Last Man Who Knew Everything*, New York/London 2004.

Frascarelli 2016
Dalma Frascarelli, *L'Arte del Dissenso. Pittura e libertinismi nell'Italia del Seicento*, Turin 2016.

Freeman Bauer 1978
Linda Freeman Bauer, "'Quanto si disegna, si dipinge ancora': Some Observations on the Development of the Oil Sketch," in *Storia dell'Arte*, vol. 32, 1978, pp. 45–57.

Freeman Bauer 1987
Linda Freeman Bauer, "Oil Sketches, Unfinished Paintings, and the Inventories of Artists' Estates," in *Light on the Eternal City: Observations and Discoveries in the Art and Architecture of Rome*, ed. Hellmut Hager and Susan Scott Munshower, University Park, P. A. 1987 (Papers in Art History from the Pennsylvania State University 2), pp. 93–103.

G

Gabburri c. 1730–1742
Francesco Maria Niccolò Gabburri, *Vite di Pittori*, c. 1730–1742, Ms. Palatino E.B. 9.5 (Biblioteca Nazionale Centrale di Firenze), I–IV, iv–c 299r, v.

Gabrielli 1955
Ada Maria Gabrielli, "Un quadro ignorato del Castiglione", in *Commentari*, vol. 6, 1955, pp. 261–266.

Griffiths 1988
Antony Griffiths, "Monotypes," in *Print Quarterly*, vol. 5, 3 (1988), pp. 56–60.

H

Haskell 1963
Francis Haskell, *Patrons and Painters: A Study in the Relations between Italian Art and Society in the Age of the Baroque*, London 1963.

Herklotz 1992
Ingo Herklotz, "Cassiano and the Christian Tradition," in *Cassiano Dal Pozzo's Paper Museum* 1, Ivrea 1992, pp. 31–48.

J

Jeutter 2004
Ewald Jeutter, "Zur Problematik der Rembrandt-Rezeption im Werk des Genuesen Giovanni Benedetto Castiglione (Genua 1609–1664 Mantua)," PhD diss., Eberhard-Karls-Universität Tübingen 2004.

K

Köhler 1891
Sylvester R. Köhler, "Das Monotyp," in *Chronik für vervielfältigende Kunst*, vol. 4, 3 (1891), pp. 17–20.

Kristeller 1912
Paul Kristeller, "Castiglione, Giovanni Bene-detto," in *Allgemeines Lexikon der Bildenden Künstler von der Antike bis zur Gegenwart*, vol. 6, Leipzig 1912, pp. 164–166.

L

Laertius 1853
Diogenes Laertius, *The Lives and Opinions of Eminent Philosophers*, trans. Charles Duke Yonge, London 1853.

Lafranconi 2003
Matteo Lafranconi, "A Roman Collector of the Late Sixteenth Century: Antonio Tronsarelli," in *The Burlington Magazine*, vol. 140, 1145 (1998), pp. 537–550, reprinted in *Collecting Prints and Drawings in Europe, 1500–1750*, ed. Caroline Elam, Christopher Baker, and Genevieve Warwick, London 2003, pp. 55–78.

Langdon 2007
Helen Langdon, "Relics of the Golden Age: The Vagabond Philosopher," in *Others and Outcasts in Early Modern Europe: Picturing the Social Margins*, ed. Tom Nichols, Aldershot 2007, pp. 157–177.

Lanzi 1809
Luigi Lanzi, *Storia pittorica della Italia: dal risorgimento delle belle arti fin presso al fine del XVIII secolo*, 6 vols., Bassano 1809.

Lavaggi 2000/2003
Andrea Lavaggi, "Oggetti preposti e soggetti posposti nella pittura del Grechetto: alcuni aspetti e significati," in *Studi di Storia delle Arti*, vol. 10 (2000/2003), pp. 237–243.

Leonardi 2013
Andrea Leonardi, *Genoese Way of Life: vivere da collezionisti tra Seicento e Settecento*, Rome 2013.

von Lorck 1967
Carl von Lorck, "Genius der Kunstlehre: Zwei Handzeichnungen von Benedetto Castiglione und François Boucher," in *Vom Geist des deutschen Ostens. Diskurse zur Kunst und Strukturanalyse des deutschen Ostens*, Berlin 1967, pp. 94–101.

Lorizzo 2010
Loredana Lorizzo, *Pellegrino Peri: Il mercato dell'arte nella Roma barocca*, Rome 2010.

Lukehart 1987
Peter Lukehart, "Contending Ideals: The Nobility of G.B. Paggi and the Nobility of Painting," PhD diss., Johns Hopkins University, 1987.

Lukehart 1993
Peter Lukehart, "Delineating the Genoese Studio: Giovani accartati or sotto padre?" in *The Artist's Workshop*, ed. Peter Lukehart, Washington, D.C. 1993, pp. 37–58.

Lukehart 2015
Peter Lukehart, "The Practice and Pedagogy of Drawing in the Accademia di San Luca," in *Lernt Zeichnen! Techniken zwischen Kunst und Wissenschaft, 1525–1925* (exh. cat. Heidelberg), ed. Maria Heilmann et al., Passau 2015, pp. 45–58.

M

Magnani 1990
Lauro Magnani, "L'adorazione dei pastori," in exh. cat. Genoa 1990, pp. 118–121 (cat. 14).

Magnani 2014
Lauro Magnani, "Giovanni Benedetto Castiglione, il Grechetto, un vedere 'filisofico,'" in *Pensiero anticonformista e libertinismo erudito nel Seicento. Il crocevia genovese*, ed. Alberto Beniscelli, Lauro Magnani, and Andrea Spiriti, Rome 2014, pp. 215–234.

Mariette 1744
Pierre-Jean Mariette, *Recueil d'estampes d'après les tableaux des peintres les plus célèbres [...] dans le Cabinet de M. Boyer d'Aguilles*, Paris 1744.

Mariette 1851–1862
Pierre-Jean Mariette, *Abcedario*, 6 vols., Paris 1851–1862.

de Marolles 1666
Michel de Marolles, *Catalogue de Livres d'Estampes et des Figures en Taille douce: avec un dénombrement des pièces qui y sont contenues*, Paris 1666.

Meroni 1971
Ubaldo Meroni (ed.), *Lettere e altri documenti intorno alla storia della pittura: Giovanni Benedetto Castiglione [...]* (Fonti per la storia della pittura 1), Genoa 1971.

Meroni 1973
Ubaldo Meroni (ed.), *Lettere e altri documenti intorno alla storia della pittura: Giovanni Benedetto Castiglione [...]* (Fonti per la storia della pittura 2), Genoa 1973.

Meroni 1978
Ubaldo Meroni (ed.), *Lettere e altri documenti intorno alla storia della pittura: Giovanni Benedetto Castiglione [...]* (Fonti per la storia della pittura e della scultura antica 8), Monzambano 1978.

Meyer 1984
Annie Meyer, "Castiglione, quêteur de lumière et inventeur du monotype," in *Revue de la Bibliothèque Nationale*, vol. 13 (automne 1984), pp. 17–24.

Miller 1994
Norbert Miller, *Archäologie des Traums. Ein Versuch über Giovanni Battista Piranesi*, Munich 1994.

Montanari 2015
Giacomo Montanari, *Libri Dipinti Statue: Rapporti e relazioni tra raccolte librarie, collezionismo e produzione artistica a Genova tra XVI e XVII secolo*, Genoa 2015.

Montanari 2020
Giacomo Montanari, "Tra 'antico sapere' e pittura 'moderna': la cultura del secolo barocco nei dipinti e nelle letture di Giovanni Benedetto Castiglione (1609–1664)," in *Letterati, artisti, mecenati del seicento e del settecento: Identità, culturali tra Antico e Moderno*, ed. Michela di Macco, Florence 2020, pp. 1–31.

N

Newcome 1981
Mary Newcome, "Drawings by Castiglione," in *Paragone*, vol. 32, 377 (1981), pp. 31–37.

Newcome 1982
Mary Newcome, "Genoese Artists in the Shadow of Castiglione," in *Paragone*, vol. 33, 391 (1982), pp. 25–36.

Newcome 1985a
Mary Newcome, "Castiglione's Teacher Giovanni Battista Paggi," in *Paragone*, vol. 36, 419–423 (1985), pp. 193–201.

Newcome 1985b
Mary Newcome, "Salvator Castiglione," in *Le dessin à Gênes du XVIe au XVIIIe siècle* (exh. cat. Paris), ed. Mary Newcome and Catherine Monbeig Goguel, Paris 1985, pp. 88–89.

Newcome 1988
Mary Newcome, "Castiglione dopo il 1650," in *Antichità Viva*, vol. 27, 3/4 (1988), pp. 26–30.

Newcome 1996
Mary Newcome, "Castiglione in the 1630s," in *Nuovi Studi*, vol. 1, 2 (1996), pp. 59–66.

Nussdorfer 1998
Laurie Nussdorfer, "Print and Pageantry in Baroque Rome," in *Sixteenth Century Journal*, vol. 29, 2 (summer 1998), pp. 439–464.

O

Orlando 2012
Anna Orlando, *Pittura fiammingo-genovese: Nature morte, ritratti e paesaggi del Seicento e primo Settecento. Ritrovamenti dal collezionismo private*, Turin 2012.

Ottley 1818
William Young Ottley, *Engravings of the Most Noble the Marquis of Stafford's Collection of Pictures*, London 1818.

P

Percy 1967
Ann Percy, "Castiglione's Chronology: Some Documentary Notes," in *The Burlington Magazine*, vol. 109 (1967), pp. 672–677.

Percy 1970
Ann Percy, "Magic and Melancholy: Castiglione's Sorceress in Hartford," in *Wadsworth Atheneum Bulletin*, vol. 6, 3 (1970), pp. 2–27.

Percy 1975
Ann Percy, "Notes on Castiglione's Monotypes," in *Print-Collector*, vol. 29, November–December 1975, pp. 73–78.

Pio 1977
Nicola Pio, *Le Vite di pittori, scultori, et architetti: (cod. ms. Capponi 257)*, ed. Catherine Enggass and Robert Enggass, Vatican City 1977.

Pissavino 1985
Paolo Pissavino, "Il cortegiano incarcerato e il palazzo della Filosofia: Immagini retoriche e politiche nel 'Carcere Illuminato' di Angelo Tarachia," in *Il Seicento nell'arte e nella cultura con riferimenti a Mantova*, Mantua 1985, pp. 31–35.

Plutarch 1914–1926
Plutarch, *Lives*, trans. B. Perrin, 11 vols., London, 1914–1926.

Pollak 1931
Oskar Pollak, *Die Kunsttätigkeit unter Urban VIII: Die Peterskirche in Rom*, Vienna 1931.

Pozzi 2021
Franco Pozzi, "Riemerge un 'monotipo' di Giovanni Battista Castiglione (detto il Grechetto), il grande innovatore dell'arte dell'incisione," URL: www.aboutartonline.com/riemerge-un-monotipo-di-giovanni-battista-castiglione-detto-il-grechetto-il-grande-innovatore-dellarte-dellincisione/ (accessed May 24, 2021).

Préaud 1990
Maxime Préaud, "Guillaume Chasteau, graveur et éditeur d'estampes à Paris (1635–1683), et la peinture italienne," in *Seicento: La peinture italienne du XVIIe siècle et la France*, Paris 1990, pp. 125–146.

Préaud 2002
Maxime Préaud, "L'inventaire après-décès de Jean Ier Leblond," in *Nouvelles de l'estampe*, vol. 182, 2002, pp. 19–37.

Puncuh 1984
Dino Puncuh, "Collezionismo e commercio di quadri nella Genova sei-settecentesca: note archivistiche dai registri contabili dei Durazzo," in *Rassegna degli Archivi di Stato*, vol. 44, 1984, pp. 164–218.

R

Ratti 1766
Carlo Giuseppe Ratti, *Istruzione di quanto può vedersi di più bello in Genova*, Genoa 1766 (1780).

Ratti 1768–1769
Carlo Giuseppe Ratti, *Delle Vite de' pittori, scultori ed architetti genovesi*, 2 vols., Genoa 1768–1769.

Raviglia 1923
Emilio Raviglia, "Tre 'prove uniche' di G.B. Castiglione," in *Bollettino d'arte*, vol. 2, 1923, pp. 419–422.

Ripa 1593
Cesare Ripa, *Iconologia overo descrittione dell'imagini universali cavate dall' antichità et da altri luoghi*, Rome 1593.

Ripa 1630
Cesare Ripa, *Della più che novissima Iconologia*, Padua 1630.

Robinson 1981
William W. Robinson, "This Passion for Prints," in *Printmaking in the Age of Rembrandt* (exh. cat. Boston), ed. C. Ackley, Boston 1981, pp. 27–48.

Röhn 1932
Franz Röhn, "Die Graphik des Giovanni Benedetto Castiglione," PhD diss., Friedrich-Wilhelms-Universität (Berlin), 1932.

Rosand 1991
Ellen Rosand, *Opera in Seventeenth-Century Venice: The Creation of a Genre*, Berkeley 1991.

Rotatori 2021
Francesco Rotatori, "Il Grechetto a Roma. Committenza, grafica, letteratura," PhD diss., Sapienza Università di Roma, 2021.

Rowlands 1996
Eliot W. Rowlands, *Italian Paintings 1300–1800*, Kansas City 1996.

Royalton-Kisch 1988
Martin Royalton-Kisch, "A Monotype by Sallaert," in *Print Quarterly*, vol. 5, 1 (1988), pp. 60–61.

Rutgers 2003
Jaco Rutgers, "La renommée de Rembrandt dans l'Italie du XVIIe siècle," in exh. cat. Épinal 2003, pp. 10–30.

Rutgers 2004
Jaco Rutgers, "Not Giovanni Benedetto but Salvatore Castiglione," in *Print Quarterly*, vol. 21, 2 (2004), pp. 163–164.

Rutgers 2008
Jaco Rutgers, "Rembrandt in Italië. Receptie en verzamelgeschiedenis," PhD diss., University of Utrecht, 2008.

S

Salerno 1970
Luciano Salerno, "Il Dissenso nella Pittura," in *Storia dell'Arte*, vol. 5, 1970, pp. 34–65.

von Sandrart 1925
Joachim von Sandrart, *Academie der Bau, Bild und Mahlerey-Künste*, ed. Arthur R. Peltzer, Munich 1925.

Santucci 1985
Paola Santucci, *Poussin: Tradizione Ermetica e Classicismo Gesuita*, Salerno 1985.

Sganzerla 2014
Anita V. Sganzerla, "Invention and Erudition in the Art of Giovanni Benedetto Castiglione: Case Studies, c. 1645–1655," PhD diss., University of London (Courtauld Institute of Art), 2014.

Sganzerla 2017
Anita V. Sganzerla, "Giovanni Benedetto Castiglione's *Temporalis Aeternitas* 1645: Early Modern Prints, Time and Memory," in *Visual Past*, vol. 4, 2017, pp. 433–467.

Snyder 2009
Jon R. Snyder, *Dissimulation and the Culture of Secrecy in Early Modern Europe*, Berkeley and London 2009.

Sohm 2001
Philip Sohm, *Style in the Art Theory of Early Modern Italy*, Cambridge 2001.

Sonnabend 2011
Martin Sonnabend, "Claude Lorrain: The Printmaker," in *Claude Lorrain: The Enchanted Landscape* (exh. cat. Oxford/Frankfurt), eds. Martina Sonnabend and John Whiteley, London 2011, pp. 137–150.

Soprani 1674
Raffaele Soprani, *Le Vite de Pittori, Scoltori, et Architetti Genovesi e de' Forastieri, che in Genoua operarono con alcuni Ritratti de gli stessi*, Genoa 1674.

Spione 2020
Gelsomina Spione, "Grechetto, un talento inquieto, tra Genova, Roma (e Napoli)," in *Napoli, Genova, Milano: Scambi artistici e culturali tra città legate alla Spagna (1610–1640)*, ed. Lauro Magnani et al., Milan 2020, pp. 321–340.

Sposato-Friedrich 2014
Ester Sposato-Friedrich, *G. B. Castiglione: Nuove proposte di lettura di un'iconografia enigmatica*, Munich 2014.

Standring 1982
Timothy J. Standring, "Genium Io: Benedicti Castilionis Ianeun: The Paintings of Giovanni Benedetto Castiglione (1609–1663/65)," PhD diss., University of Chicago, 1982.

Standring 1987a
Timothy J. Standring, "Giovanni Benedetto Castiglione," in *La Pittura a Genova e in Liguria*, ed. Colette Bozzo Dufour, vol. 2, Genoa 1987, pp. 158–161.

Standring 1987b
Timothy J. Standring, "Giovanni Benedetto Castiglione," in *Print Quarterly*, vol. 4, 1 (1987), pp. 65–73.

Standring 1990
Timothy J. Standring, "Castiglione i Nàpols," in *Nàpols i el Barroc Mediterrani* (exh. cat. Valencia), ed. Joaquim Horta, Barcelona 1990, pp. 38–39.

Standring 1997
Timothy J. Standring, "Giovanni Benedetto Castiglione detto il Grechetto (dit le Grechetto)," in *Genua tempu fà*, Monaco 1997, pp. 77–84.

Standring 2000
Timothy J. Standring, "An Exclusive Artist 'Conventio' between Giovanni Benedetto Castiglione and Desiderio de Ferrari," in *Studi di storia dell'arte in onore di Denis Mahon*, ed. Maria Grazia Bernardini, Silvia Danesi Squarzina, and Claudio Strinati, Milan 2000, pp. 259–262.

Standring 2001
Timothy J. Standring, "L'Adoration des Bergers, 1659, par Giovanni Benedetto Castiglione au Musée du Louvre," in *Revue du Louvre*, vol. 2, 2001, pp. 43–54.

Standring 2011a
Timothy J. Standring, "Giovanni Benedetto Castiglione, Circe Changing the Companions of Ulysses into Boars," in *Old Master & 19th Century Paintings, Drawings & Watercolors*, Christie's, New York, 26 January 2011, lot 41.

Standring 2011b
Timothy J. Standring, "Giovanni Benedetto Castiglione, Jacob's Journey," in *Old Master & 19th Century Paintings, Drawings & Watercolors*, Christie's, New York, 26 January 2011, lot 50.

Standring 2012
Timothy J. Standring, "The Creation of Adam," in *Capturing the Sublime: Italian Drawings of the Renaissance and Baroque*, ed. Suzanne Folds McCullagh, New Haven 2012, pp. 172–173, 287.

Standring 2021
Timothy J. Standring, "Giovanni Benedetto Castiglione's Versions of the Allegory of Vanity," in *Close Reading. Kunsthistorische Interpretationen vom Mittelalter bis zur Moderne*, ed. Stefan Albl, Berthold Hub, and Anna Frasca-Rath, Berlin 2021, pp. 482–490.

Stoesser 2018
Alison Stoesser, *Van Dyck's Hosts in Genoa: Lucas and Cornelis de Wael's Lives, Business Activities and Works*, 2 vols., Turnhout 2018.

Suhr 2010
Norbert Suhr, "Der Genius des Castiglione – Versuch einer Interpretation," in *Roma Quanta Fuit. Beiträge zur Architektur-, Kunst-, und Kulturgeschichte von der Antike bis zur Gegenwart*, ed. Albert Dietl et al., Augsburg 2010, pp. 551–562.

Suida-Manning 1984
Bertina Suida-Manning, "The Transformation of Circe: The Significance of the Sorceress as Subject in 17th-century Genoese Painting," in *Scritti di storia dell'arte in onore di Federico Zeri*, Milan 1984, pp. 689–707.

Summers 1981
David Summers, *Michelangelo and the Language of Art*, Princeton 1981.

Suthor 2021
Nicola Suthor, *Bravura: Virtuosity and Ambition in Early Modern European Painting*, Princeton 2021.

T

Tanner 2015
Paul Tanner, "The Tradition of the Monotype and Andy Warhol's *Blotted-Line*," in *Andy Warhol. The Life Years 1949–1959* (exh. cat. Zurich), ed. Graphische Sammlung ETH Zürich, Munich 2015, pp. 10–15.

Thuillier 1979
Jacques Thuillier, "Un chef-d'œuvre de François Perrier au Musée des Beaux-Arts de Rennes: Les Adieux de saint Pierre et de saint Paul," in *Bulletin des Amis du Musée de Rennes*, vol. 3, 1979, pp. 53–65.

Tiberia 2005
Vitaliano Tiberia, *La compagnia di S. Giuseppe di Terrasanta da Gregoria XV a Innocenzo XII*, Lecce 2005.

Tsai 2008
Min-Ling Tsai, "Giovanni Benedetto Castigliones *biblico viaggio patriarcale: genere minore* oder *istoria*? Pastorale Motivik als Mittel zur Darstellung der Gattungsproblematik," PhD diss., Freie Universität zu Berlin, 2008.

Turner 1987
Nicholas Turner, "A Castiglione Unjustly Demoted," in *Print Quarterly*, vol. 4 (June 1987), pp. 418–419.

V

Vazzoler 1991–1994
Franco Vazzoler, "'… anche dagli scogli nascon pennelli …': Luca Assarino e i pittori genovesi del Seicento. Le Dediche degli Argomenti dei Giuochi di Fortuna, 1655," in *Studi di storia delle arti*, vol. 7, 1991–1994, pp. 35–61.

Volpi 2010
Caterina Volpi, "The Great Theatre of the World: Salvator Rosa and the Academies," in *Salvator Rosa* (exh. cat. London/Fort Worth), ed. Helen Langdon, London 2010, pp. 51–73.

Volpi 2014
Caterina Volpi, *Salvator Rosa (1615–1673): "Pittore Famoso,"* Rome 2014.

W

Wallace 1965
Richard W. Wallace, "The Genius of Salvator Rosa," in *Art Bulletin*, vol. 47, 4 (1965), pp. 471–480.

Wallace 1979
Richard W. Wallace, *The Etchings of Salvator Rosa*, Princeton 1979.

Watelet/Levesque 1792
Claude-Henri Watelet and Pierre Ch. Levesque, *Dictionnaire des arts de peinture, sculpture et gravure*, 5 vols., Paris 1792.

Waterhouse 1967
Ellis Waterhouse, "An Immaculate Conception by G. B. Castiglione," in *Minneapolis Institute of Arts Bulletin*, vol. 56, 1967, pp. 5–10.

Welsh Reed 1989
Sue Welsh Reed, "Giovanni Benedetto Castiglione," *Italian Etchers of the Renaissance and Baroque* (exh. cat. Boston), ed. Sue Welsh Reed and Richard W. Wallace, Boston 1989, pp. 262–271.

Welsh Reed 1991
Sue Welsh Reed, "Giovanni Benedetto Castiglione's God Creating Adam: The First Masterpiece in Monotype Medium," in *Museum-Studies*, vol. 17, 1 (1991), pp. 66–73.

Whiteley 1998
Jon J. L. Whiteley, *Claude Lorrain: Drawings from the Collections of the British Museum and the Ashmolean Museum*, London 1998.

Wittkower 1955
Rudolf Wittkower, *Gian Lorenzo Bernini: The Sculptor of the Roman Baroque*, London 1955.

Wittkower 1967
Rudolf Wittkower, "Introduction," in *Masters of the Loaded Brush: Oil Sketches from Rubens to Tiepolo* (exh. cat. New York), ed. Columbia University, Department of Art History and Archaeology, New York 1967, pp. 15–25.

Woodall 2003
Joanna Woodall, "Drawing in Color," in *Peter Paul Rubens, a Touch of Brilliance: Oil Sketches and Related Works from the State Hermitage Museum and the Courtauld Institute Gallery* (exh. cat. London), Munich 2003, pp. 9–21.

Wootton 1997
Astrid Wootton, "On Circe's Island: Subversive Power Relationships in a Painting by Sinibaldo Scorza," in *Melbourne Art Journal*, vol. 1, 1997, pp. 17–24.

Wootton 1998
Astrid Wootton, "Sinibaldo Scorza (1589–1631): A Landscape Painter in Genoa and Savoy in the Early Seventeenth Century," PhD diss., University of Melbourne, 1998.

Exhibition Catalogs

Exh. cat. Binghamton/Worcester 1972
Genoese Baroque Drawings (Binghamton University Art Museum/Worcester Art Museum), ed. Mary Newcome Schleier, Binghamton 1972.

Exh. cat. Cologne 2014
Der Abklatsch. Eine Kunst für sich (Wallraf-Richartz-Museum, Cologne), ed. Thomas Ketelsen, Cologne 2014.

Exh. cat. Cologne/Zurich/Vienna 1996
Das Capriccio als Kunstprinzip. Zur Vorgeschichte der Moderne von Arcimboldo und Callot bis Tiepolo und Goya (Wallraf-Richartz-Museum, Cologne/Kunsthaus Zürich/Kunsthistorisches Museum im Palais Harrach, Vienna), ed. Ekkehard Mai, Milan 1996.

Exh. cat. Dresden 2019
Rembrandts Strich (Kupferstich-Kabinett, Staatliche Kunstsammlungen Dresden), ed. Stephanie Buck and Jürgen Müller, London 2019.

Exh. cat. Épinal 2003
Rembrandt et les peintres-graveurs italiens de Castiglione à Tiepolo (Musée départemental d'art ancien et contemporain à Épinal), ed. Matthieu Gilles, Bozena Anna Kowalczyk, and Jaco Rutgers, Brussels 2003.

Exh. cat. Florence 1989
Disegni genovesi dal XVI al XVIII secolo (Galleria degli Uffizi, Florence), ed. Mary Newcome Schleier, Florence 1989.

Exh. cat. Frankfurt/Fort Worth/Richmond/Edinburgh 1989–1990
The Consul Smith Collection: Masterpieces of Italian Drawings from the Royal Library, Windsor Castle (Schirn Kunsthalle, Frankfurt/Kimbell Art Museum, Fort Worth/Virginia Museum of Arts, Richmond/National Gallery of Scotland, Edinburgh), ed. Frances Vivian, Munich 1989.

Exh. cat. Genoa 1990
Il Genio di Giovanni Benedetto Castiglione il Grechetto (Accademia Ligustica di Belle Arti, Genoa), ed. Gianvittorio Dillon, Genoa 1990.

Exh. cat. London/Denver/Fort Worth 2013
Castiglione: Lost Genius (The Queen's Gallery, London/Denver Art Museum/Kimbell Art Museum, Fort Worth), ed. Timothy J. Standring and Martin Clayton, London 2013.

Exh. cat. Milan 1982
L'Opera incisa di Giovanni Benedetto Castiglione (Sala delle Asse, Castello Sforzesco, Milan), ed. Paolo Bellini, Milan 1982.

Exh. cat. Munich 2004
Werke von und um Giovanni Benedetto Castiglione (Pinakothek der Moderne, Munich), ed. Kurt Zeitler, Munich 2004.

Exh. cat. New York 1996
Genoa: Drawings and Prints 1530–1800 (Metropolitan Museum of Art, New York), ed. Carmen Bambach and Nadine M. Orenstein, New York 1996.

Exh. cat. New York/Boston 1980
The Painterly Print: Monotypes from the Seventeenth to the Twentieth Century (Metropolitan Museum of Art, New York/Museum of Fine Arts, Boston), ed. Colta Ives et al., New York 1980.

Exh. cat. Philadelphia 1971
Giovanni Benedetto Castiglione: Master Draughtsman of the Italian Baroque (Philadelphia Museum of Art), ed. Ann Percy, Philadelphia 1971.

Exh. cat. Turin 2018
Le invenzioni di Grechetto (Galleria Sabauda, Turin), ed. Annamaria Bava, Giorgio Careddu, and Gelsomina Spione, Genoa 2018.

Exh. cat. Washington/Rome 2020
A Superb Baroque: Art in Genoa, 1600–1750 (National Gallery of Art, Washington, D.C./Scuderie del Quirinale, Rome), ed. Jonathan Bober, Piero Boccardo, and Franco Boggero, Princeton 2020.

Photo Credits

Detail Views

Colophon

This book is published in conjunction
with the exhibition

*Baroque Brilliance – Drawings and
Prints by Giovanni Benedetto Castiglione*
Kunsthaus Zürich
December 10, 2021 – March 6, 2022

Exhibition

Curators: Jonas Beyer,
Timothy J. Standring

Project assistant and organization:
Martina Ciardelli

Coordination: Franziska Lentzsch

Indemnity and transportation:
Nora Gassner

Communication and marketing:
Björn Quellenberg and team

Sponsorship and Fundraising:
Jacqueline Greenspan

Conservation: Rebecca Honold

Typography: Lena Huber

Technical support: Robert Sulzer and team

Art education: Sibyl Kraft and team

Publication

Published by Zürcher Kunstgesellschaft /
Kunsthaus Zürich

Concept: Jonas Beyer,
Timothy J. Standring

Editing: Jonas Beyer, Martina Ciardelli,
Timothy J. Standring

Catalog management: Martina Ciardelli

Coordination: Franziska Lentzsch

Translations (German-English):
Carola Kleinstück-Schulman, Ian Pepper,
Büro LS Anderson

Copy editing: Lance Anderson,
Büro LS Anderson

Graphic design: Nele Bielenberg,
Annett Stoy, Sandstein Verlag

Typesetting: Christian Werner,
Sandstein Verlag

Pre-press and reproduction:
Jana Neumann, Sandstein Verlag

Production: Katrin Hoyer, Sandstein Verlag

Printing and binding:
FINIDR s. r. o., Cĕský Tĕšín

Typeface: Demos Next Pro
Paper: Profi Silk

Produced and distributed by
Sandstein Verlag
www.sandstein-verlag.de

ISBN 978-3-95498-642-2 (English)
ISBN 978-3-95498-631-6 (German)

Supported by

KYTHERA
KULTUR-STIFTUNG
Düsseldorf

WOLFGANG RATJEN STIFTUNG
Vaduz

T A V O L O Z Z A
F O U N D A T I O N

as well as another foundation
which prefers to remain
unmentioned.